THE UNOFFICIAL

Dunder Mifflin

ACTIVITY BOOK

Quizzes, Trivia, Word Searches, Crosswords, Mazes, & More From America's Favorite Workplace

WELCOME TO DUNDER MIFFLIN!

Whether you are here from Stamford, Utica, Nashua, or you are Mr. or Mrs. Outside Hire, we welcome you. If we were there at the Scranton branch, we would offer you a c-shaped bagel or perhaps a metal water bottle of orange juice. In any case, we are happy to have you join us.

In the following pages, you will be introduced to your coworkers. Some of them are real characters. Go on some sales calls, attend parties planned by the PPC, and sit through some conference room meetings. You will learn more about your coworkers and this knowledge will help you solve the puzzles in this book. Some of the answers will feel easy, like any junior salesman would get them. Others will test your knowledge. If you succeed, you might earn your blackbelt in Dunder Mifflin trivia! Fail, and you'll be sent to the annex.

Now, stop acting like an idiot, and get to work!

-Corporate

TABLE OF CONTENTS

Mini Quiz #1

1. What is not a pretzel day topping?
   A. cotton candy bits
   B. chocolate chips
   C. toffee nuts
   D. butterscotch bits
   E. sprinkles

2. What does Angela call her grandmother?
   A. Grandmudder
   B. MeeMaw
   C. Nana Mimi
   D. Gamma
   E. Nona

3. Who is not an accountant?
   A. Creed
   B. Angela
   C. Kevin
   D. Oscar

4. Where does Jan's sister live?
   A. Sedona
   B. Flagstaff
   C. Phoenix
   D. Scottsdale
   E. Tucson

5. Who did Dwight play in the 7th grade production of "Oklahoma!"?
   A. Quiet Quaker
   B. Silent Salesman
   C. Hushy the Handyman
   D. unspeaking usher
   E. Mutey the Mailman

6. What is the name of the exercise equipment Dwight sits on?
   A. yoga ball
   B. exercise sphere
   C. health spherule
   D. strength globe
   E. fitness orb

7. Who wins the hot dog eating contest?
   A. Andy
   B. Stanley
   C. Kevin
   D. Creed
   E. Meredith

Mini Quiz #2

1. What is the name of Kevin's ex-fiance?
   A. Macy
   B. Stacy
   C. Tracey
   D. Jacey
   E. Kacey

2. What does Michael yell from the front of the Booze Cruise?
   A. Let's get drunk!
   B. Screw you Captain Jack!
   C. I'm the Party Captain too!
   D. I'm King of the World!
   E. Dwight you ignorant slut!

3. What is a nate-pon?
   A. Coupon from Nate for things like tickles and gum
   B. A rock that gets stuck on the bottom of your shoe
   C. Dwight's favorite Pennsylvania Dutch confection
   D. Its actually Nate-pong, and its where Nate bounces back and forth between Jim and Pam's desk

4. Who is not a character in the murder mystery game?
   A. Nathaniel Nutmeg
   B. Caleb Crawdad
   C. Min T. Julep
   D. Deborah U. Tante
   E. Beatrix Bourbon

5. What is the worst part about prison?
   A. the watercolor classes were subpar
   B. the rec room tv was too small
   C. the business classes weren't accredited
   D. too little outdoors time
   E. the dementors

6. What does Dwight find under the seat of Meredith's mini van?
   A. bottle of alcohol
   B. pack of condoms
   C. a joint
   D. a gun
   E. her wig

7. Who went missing from Phyllis' wedding?
   A. Michael
   B. Uncle Al
   C. Bob Vance
   D. Elroy
   E. Creed

Mini Quiz #3

1. What is the most important thing to do when a new baby is born?
   A. make sure it gets sufficient beet to skin contact
   B. play it "For the Longest Time" by William Joel on your recorder
   C. give it paper clips
   D. mark it secretly in a kind of a mark that only you could recognize and no baby snatcher can ever copy

2. What vehicle served as Phyllis and Bob's wedding getaway car?
   A. yellow cab
   B. A Vance Refridgeration Work Vehicle
   C. golf cart
   D. Phyllis' PT Cruiser

3. What is not a way that Michael has come close to hurting himself?
   A. Jumping off a multi-story building
   B. Firing a gun in the office
   C. Throwing scissors
   D. Eating poison mushrooms

4. Who does not go to Pam's art show?
   A. Toby
   B.Michael
   C. Oscar
   D. Roy
   E. Gil

5. What is not a text read by the Finer Things Club?
   A. Lolita
   B. Room with a View
   C. Angela's Ashes
   D. Memoirs of a Geisha

6. What is Gabe said to be afraid of?
   A. the sun
   B. flying
   C. hugs
   D. the baler

7. Why was Dwight shunned by his family as a child?
   A. For accusing his parents of making up the Belschnickel
   B. For not collecting the goose eggs for Sunday supper
   C. He gave Mose a blackeye while fighting over who got the stink sac
   D. He failed to save the excess oil from a can of tuna
   E. He stole money from his mother to get a haircut by a real barber

Mini Quiz #4

1. What was the movie that inspired Movie Mondays?
    A. Varsity Blues
    B. The Princess Bride
    C. Cookie Monster sings Chocolate Rain
    D. Threat Level Midnight
    E. The Devil Wears Prada

2. What did Micheal sell at his telemarketing job?
    A. vacuums
    B. time shares
    C. cable packages
    D. diet pills

3. Who has Kelly not kissed?
    A. Darryl
    B. Dwight
    C. Andy
    D. Ryan

4. What costume does Carol wear to Diwali?
    A. cheerleader
    B. ballerina
    C. lifeguard
    D. cowgirl
    E. chef

5. What romantic comedy does Kelly mention when she describes how Netflix works?
    A. Sweet Home Alabama
    B. Love Actually
    C. How to Lose a Guy in 10 Days
    D. Bridget Jones Diary

6. What is not an ingredient in Michael's birthday subs?
    A. tomato
    B. bologna
    C. ketchup
    D. black olives

7. What is not one of the group names on Beach Day?
    A. Ryan's Team
    B. Gryffindor
    C. Voldemort
    D. The Blue Team
    E. Team USA

Mini Quiz #5

1. How long were Ryan and Kelly married?
   A. an hour
   B. a day
   C. a week
   D. a month

2. What state does Kelly move to that Ryan also decides to move to "for unrelated reasons"?
   A. Iowa
   B. Oregon
   C. Idaho
   D. Ohio
   E. Illinois

3. On the eve of what holiday do Kelly and Ryan first hook up?
   A. Christmas
   B. Valentine's Day
   C. Diwali
   D. Halloween

4. What did Ryan do at Dwight's wedding so he could talk to Kelly?
   A. give his baby an allergic reaction
   B. interupted the wedding ceremony
   C. drove Ravi's car into a cornfield
   D. slashed her tires
   E. started a fire

5. What does the line "Kapoor and kadesperate" refer to?
   A. Kelly's time in juvi
   B. how Ryan discribes himself when he is without Kelly
   C. Kelly's line of shoes she designs
   D. opening lines of a poem Ryan writes about Kelly

6. Why does Ryan call Kelly in the middle of the night?
   A. he needs help studying for business school
   B. to use her like an object
   C. he has trouble sleeping and she will read him poetry over the phone
   D. he wants her opinion on some hats in his online shopping cart
   E. he thinks there is a murderer in his apartment

7. Why do Ryan and Kelly get divorced?
   A. Ryan gets Jan's old job at corporate
   B. Kelly's minority executive program took too much of her attention away from Ryan
   C. Ryan says he doesn't want to be married until everyone can be married
   D. Kelly's parents don't approve of Ryan

Mini Quiz #6

1. Where was William Charles Snyder born?
    A. California
    B. Florida
    C. Maine
    D. Pennsylvania
    E. Illinois

2. What does Kelly want to name her future baby?
    A. Fergie Arcade Fire Howard
    B. Usher Jennifer Hudson Kapoor
    C. Rhianna Kanye West Kapoor
    D. Avril Lavigne Kapoor-Howard

3. When Meredith contracts rabies, what is not an animal that has bitten her recently?
    A. bat
    B. rat
    C. squirrel
    D. raccoon

4. What does it say on Mose's shirt when he is about to wrestle Ryan in the barn?
    A. "Beets"
    B. "From Dwight"
    C. "Mose"
    D. "Ryan"
    E. "Fear"

5. What is Michael's ringtone?
    A. Hollaback Girl
    B. My Humps
    D. Disco Inferno
    E. Gold Digger

6. What two animals were seen engaging in an unspeakable act on the paper with the obscene watermark?
    A. duck + mouse
    B. mouse + cat
    C. dog + squirrel
    D. duck + dog
    E. cat + squirrel

7. What is the name of Andy's part time frozen yogurt chef girlfriend?
    A. Molly
    B. Jessie
    C. Morgan
    D. Jamie
    E. Maggie

This or That #1

Circle your choice:

THIS	THAT
No panties on Casual Friday	No socks on Casual Friday.
Eat a gourmet hotdog	Have a chicken breast with milk.
WUPHF.com	Suck It
Josh at Stamford	Karen at Utica
Dwight's Gym for Muscles	The Sesame Avenue Daycare Center for Infants and Toddlers
Mama Sally's Homemade Pesto	Señor Chico's Hot Cha Cha Salsa
Throwing rocks in the quarry with Creed	Wrestling cousin Mose to the ground
Philip Lipton	Philip Schrute
Pam with glasses	Meredith without a wig
Jo's dogs who dont know they're brothers	Dwight's porcupine Henrietta

"Sometimes I'll start a sentence and I don't even know where it's going. I just hope I find it along the way."

Fill in the Blank #1

Complete the quote.

1. _____ is raining from the ceilings. _____!

2. I sprout _____ _____ on a damp paper towel in my desk drawer. Very nutritious. But they smell like _____

3. It has to be official, and it has to be _____.

4. Why tip someone for a job I'm capable of doing myself? I can deliver food. I can drive a taxi. I can, and do, cut my own _____. I did, however, tip my urologist, because... I am unable to _____ my own _____.

5. Yes, it is true. I, _____ _____ am signing up with an online dating service. Thousands of people have done it, and I am going to do it. I need a username. And... I have a great one.

   _____ _____ _____

6. _____ is not allowed to talk until after he buys me a _____ Those are the rules of jinx, and they are unflinchingly rigid.

7. I wake up every morning in a bed that's too _____ drive my daughter to a school that's too _____ and then I go to work to a job for which I get _____ too little, but on _____ Day? Well, I like _____ day.

8. Please don't throw _____ at me.

9. I want the job. I really do. It's just, the rest of my family's in the _____ _____ right now. I'm supposed to be in the _____ _____ right now. I told them I was on a hike; snuck away to do this interview. I gotta get back pretty soon; they'll worry. People disappear in the _____ _____

10. I just think it's insulting that Jan thinks we need this. And, apparently, judging from her _____ Jan aspires to be a _____.

11. Bob Vance, _____ _____.

little	kidney Jim	lakes
death	poop	whore
urine	garbage	finger
beans	small hair	kid
Michael	Vance	Scott
outfit	coke	mung
refrigeration		pulverize
expensive	poop	pretzel
paid	lakes finger	finger
lakes	stones	pretzel
	lover	

Fill in the Blank #2

Complete Dwight's speech

_____ alone moves the wheels of _____! Have you ever asked yourselves in an hour of _____, which everyone finds during the day. How long we have been striving for greatness? Not only the years we've been at war, the war of _____, but from the moment as a child when we realized that the world could be conquered. It has been a lifetime's struggle. A never-ending fight. I say to you and you'll understand that it is a _____ to _____! We are _____! Salesman of Northeastern _____, I ask you once more rise and be worthy of this historical hour! No _____ is worth anything unless it can defend itself. Some people will tell you _____ is a bad word. They'll conjure up images of used car dealers and door to door _____. This is our duty – to change their perception. I say salesmen... and _____ of the world unite! We must never acquiesce for it is together, TOGETHER, THAT WE PREVAIL! We must never cede control of the _____! For it is together that we prevail!

motherland	meditation
women	privilege history
salesman	work
charlatans	fight blood
revolution	Pennsylvania
	warriors

Fill in the Blank #3

Complete the lyrics from these classic songs.

1. bye, bye, miss _____ _____ lady

2. you took my by the _____ made me a _____ that one _____

3. my horn can _____ the sky!

4. I dont wanna _____ I just wanna bang on this _____ all day

5. Hey Mr. Scott, whatcha gonna do, whatcha gonna do make our _____ _____ _____

6. Learn your rules, you better learn your rules, if you don't, you'll be _____ in your _____

7. You meet some _____ you tie some _____

8. Lazy _____ the Electric City they call it that 'cause of the _____

9. The city's laid out from east to _____ and our public _____ and libraries are truly the _____

10. Call _____ _____ if you're bit by a spider, but check that it's covered by your healthcare provider

11. Plenty of space in the parking lot, but the _____ _____ go in the _____ spot!

best night poison
dreams parks cars
work yarn west sleep
eaten come true hand
electricity man compact
control pierce little
Scranton mug model
friends chair

Fill in the Blank #4

Boom, roasted.

Pam	Andy	Angela
Kevin	Jim	Gumby
Oscar	America	Creed
everybody	Meredith	
Stanley	Oscar	Dwight

1. _____ you're 6'11 and you weigh 90 pounds, _____ has a better body than you.

2. _____ you're a kiss ass. Boom. Roasted.

3. _____ you failed art school. Boom. Roasted.

4. _____ you've slept with so many guys you're starting to look lik one.

5. _____ I can't decide between a fat joke and a dumb joke.

6. _____ your teeth called, your breath stinks.

7. Where's _____? Whoa there you are, I didn't see you there behind that grain of rice.

8. _____ you crush your wife during sex and your heart sucks.

9. _____ you're gay.

10. _____ Cornell called, they think you suck. And you're gayer tha _____!

11. Alright _____ you know I kid, you know I kid. You guys are the reason I went into the paper business, so, uh, goodnight, God bless, God bless _____ and get home safe.

Fill in the Blank #5

1. No Dwight, not the good _____ _____. People are going to get mad.

2. _____. Great equalizer.

3. "Guys, _____! It's what's for dinner! Who wants some _____ _____? "I do! I want some _____ _____!

4. No _____! Just... eat it. Eat it, Phyllis. Dip it in the water so it will slide down your gullet more easily.

5. Somebody making _____?

6. And we are spoiled because we throw out perfectly good _____ because it has a little tiny hair on it.

7. Last night I ordered a _____ by myself and I ate it over the sink like a rat.

8. I am on the third day of my cleanse diet. All I have to do is drink _____ _____ lemon juice, _____ _____ and water for all three meals.

9. It's never too early for ice cream, Jim. But we didn't have any _____ _____ so this is _____ and black _____.

10. Yes, I can do that. For, um, for two _____ we'd probably need about what 20... $20? Or $25? $20?

11. I just want to lie on the beach and eat _____ _____. That's all I've ever wanted.

12. I'll make a reservation. No, no. Let me cook for you. _____ and noodles. Baked _____ on the side.

13. Oh Angela, those _____ have _____ in them and I think Kevin's allergic to _____. You're allergic to _____ right Kevin?

tiramisu	pizza	syrup
hot	soup dogs	peanut
potato	walnuts	pepper
beef	pizza	brownies
cayenne	cauliflower	
man	walnuts	cream
	butter meat	
	mayonnaise mustard	
walnuts	ice man	tacos
maple	olives	meat

Fill in the Blank #6

1. Nobody ever helped me. I had to do it myself. Even the _____ _____ _____.

2. I want my sugar free _____ and then I want a _____ cookie.

3. It's um, it's really for anybody with a dream and a belief in _____ and a little extra time after _____

4. Please don't _____ me Michael.

5. Nah, I wouldn't have done it if it wasn't for the discount _____ There's not a lot of _____ in those _____

6. She's been sick for some time. Thank you for asking, no one asks about _____.

7. Eventually he'll figure it out, when their kids have giant heads and _____ teeth.

8. I want pie. I want _____ pie.

9. I feel _____ today. Felt much _____ yesterday. Like Benjamin Button in reverse.

10. Oh, hello Mater. Good news: I've married. _____ _____.

---

smell know sugar
doctor Fater stronger
weak fruit sprinkles
paper peach tell
looms beet-stained
magic didn't school
cookie

Jumble #1: Last Names

Unscramble each of the clue words.
Copy the letters in the circled cells to unscramble one more last name.

palrem

atniremz

hustrce

imrnta

drohaw

poaokr

beylsee

nlipbih

octst

ecnva

ahtrelp

readrbn

btnator

neomal

"Would I rather be feared or loved? Easy. Both. I want people to be afraid of how much they love me."

Jumble #2: Michael Scott

Unscramble each of the clue words.
Copy the letters in the numbered cells to other cells with the same number.

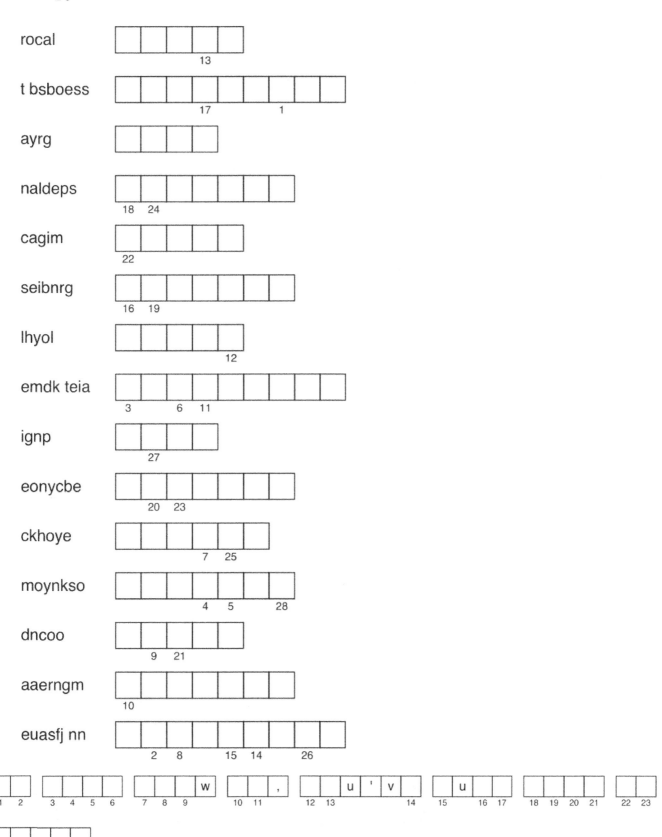

rocal

⬜⬜⬜⬜⬜
　　　　13

t bsboess

⬜⬜⬜⬜⬜⬜⬜⬜⬜
　　　17　　　1

ayrg

⬜⬜⬜⬜

naldeps

⬜⬜⬜⬜⬜⬜⬜
18　24

cagim

⬜⬜⬜⬜⬜
22

seibnrg

⬜⬜⬜⬜⬜⬜⬜
16　19

lhyol

⬜⬜⬜⬜⬜
　　　　12

emdk teia

⬜⬜⬜⬜⬜⬜⬜⬜⬜
3　　　6　11

ignp

⬜⬜⬜⬜
27

eonycbe

⬜⬜⬜⬜⬜⬜⬜
20　23

ckhoye

⬜⬜⬜⬜⬜⬜
　　　　7　25

moynkso

⬜⬜⬜⬜⬜⬜⬜
　　　4　5　　28

dncoo

⬜⬜⬜⬜⬜
　　9　21

aaerngm

⬜⬜⬜⬜⬜⬜⬜
10

euasfj nn

⬜⬜⬜⬜⬜⬜⬜⬜
　2　8　　15　14　　26

Y⬜⬜ ⬜⬜⬜⬜ ⬜⬜W ⬜⬜⬜, ⬜⬜u'v ⬜u⬜ ⬜⬜⬜⬜ ⬜⬜
1　2　　3　4　5　6　7　8　9　10　11　12　13　　14　15　16　17　18　19　20　21　22　23

⬜⬜⬜⬜⬜.
24　25　26　27　28

"There's something about an underdog that really inspires the unexceptional."

Jumble #3: Robert California

Unscramble each of the clue words.
Copy the letters in the numbered cells to other cells with the same number.

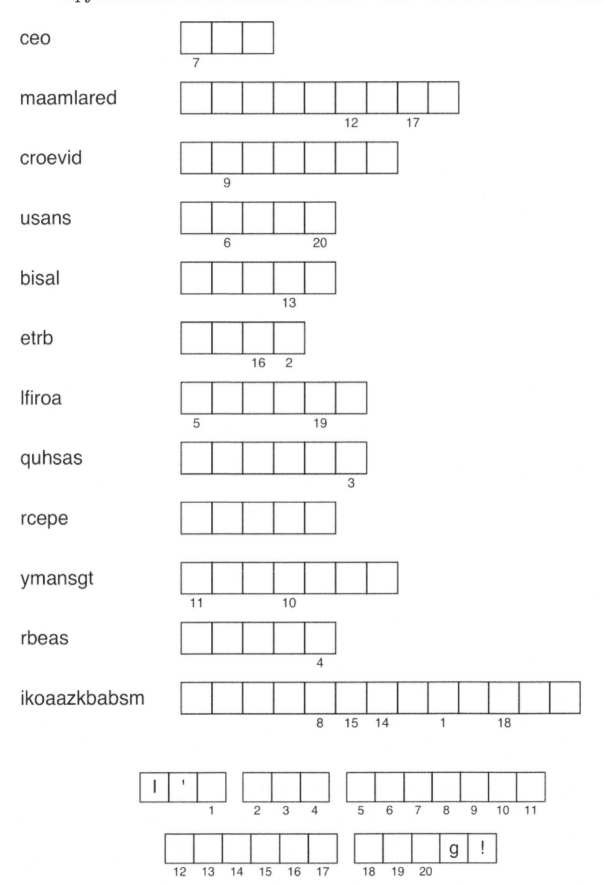

ceo

maamlared

croevid

usans

bisal

etrb

lfiroa

quhsas

rcepe

ymansgt

rbeas

ikoaazkbabsm

"I feel God in this Chili's tonight."

Jumble #4: Oscar Martinez

Unscramble each of the clue words.
Copy the letters in the circled cells to unscramble one more Oscar word.

s keitcae

ogay

xelsu

ooyl

y wgouesurhea

lg

mecinxa

evnki

thsngur bilcief

gay

omrctde

mla

atarlni

tantucacn

nesoa

"I have a lot of questions. Number one, how dare you?"

Jumble #5: The Dinner Party

Unscramble each of the clue words.
Copy the letters in the circled cells to unscramble a memorable phrase.

lsdncea

wnei

ooubscso

maslap

ceribyelt

ieuddn

babe

etnogiah htnt

odnco

dodeflo

clpoie

| | k | | | | | | | | - | | r | | |

"I am fast. To give you a reference point. I'm somewhere between a snake and a mongoose. And a panther."

Jumble #6: Andy Bernard

Unscramble each of the clue words.
Copy the letters in the circled cells to unscramble a memorable phrase.

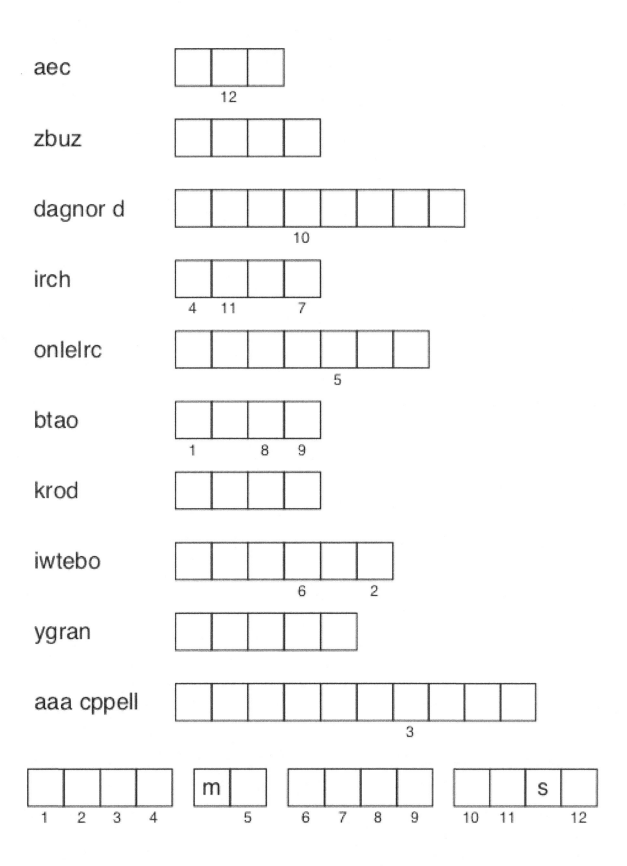

aec

zbuz

dagnor d
10

irch
4 11 7

onlelrc
5

btao
1 8 9

krod

iwtebo
6 2

ygran

aaa cppell
3

1 2 3 4 | m 5 | 6 7 8 9 | 10 11 s 12

"Sorry I annoyed you with my friendship."

Jumble #7: Gabe Lewis

Unscramble each of the clue words.
Copy the letters in the circled cells to unscramble a memorable phrase.

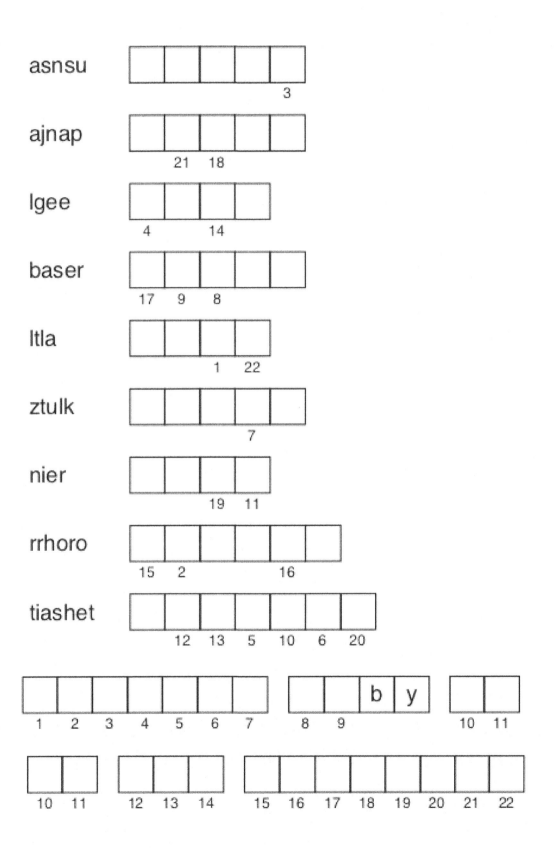

asnsu

3

ajnap

21   18

lgee

4   14

baser

17   9   8

ltla

1   22

ztulk

7

nier

19   11

rrhoro

15   2   16

tiashet

12   13   5   10   6   20

| 1 | 2 | 3 | 4 | 5 | 6 | 7 | | 8 | 9 | b | y | | 10 | 11 |

| 10 | 11 | | 12 | 13 | 14 | | 15 | 16 | 17 | 18 | 19 | 20 | 21 | 22 |

"Whenever I'm about to do something, I think, 'Would an idiot do that?' And if they would, I do not do that thing."

Jumble #8: Nellie Bertram

Unscramble each of the clue words.
Copy the letters in the circled cells to unscramble a memorable phrase.

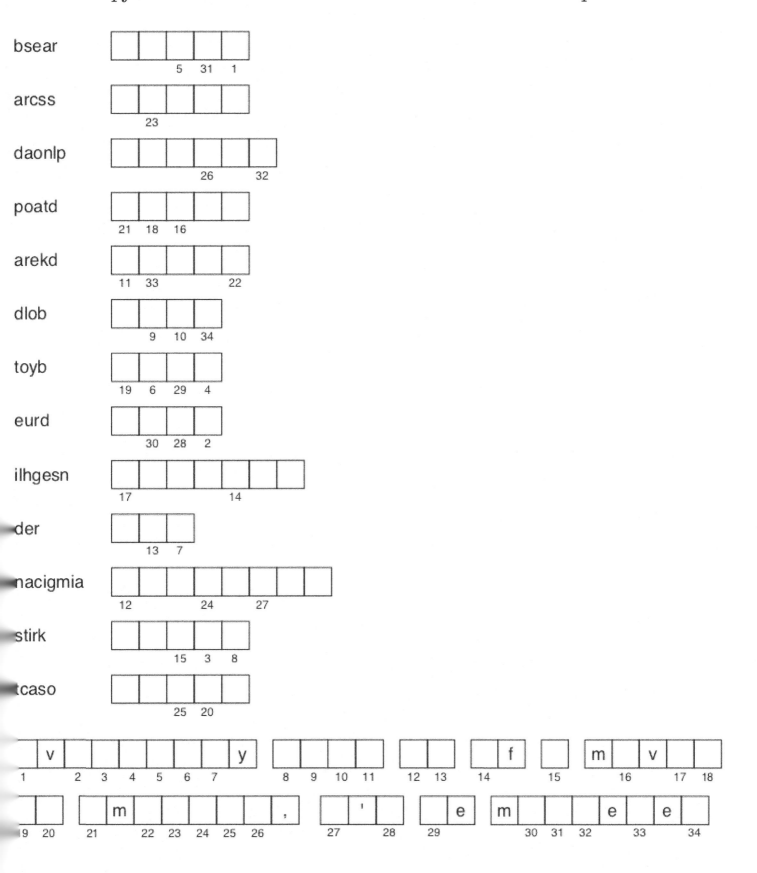

bsear

arcss

daonlp

poatd

arekd

dlob

toyb

eurd

ilhgesn

der

nacigmia

stirk

tcaso

This or That #2

Circle your choice:

THIS	THAT
Never be able to watch "The Dinner Party" again.	Never have to watch "Scott's Tots" again.
Eat a C-shaped bagel with Charles Miner.	Share a blue-blast flavored drink with Katie the purse girl.
Find out how Creed lost a toe.	Lay down for 60 seconds on the floor of Meredith's minivan.
Try Dwight's hog maw.	Eat Kevin's chili.
Have a guest appearance on Fundle Bundle.	Win the Jethro Tull Box set from Rock 107.
Work out using Dwight's fitness orb.	Work out by biking to work, like Josh at the Stanford branch.
Be the Safety Officer.	Head the Party Planning Committee
Have Stanley whittle you into a bird carving.	Have Phyllis knit you custom oven mitts.
See-saw with Mose.	Create "soundscapes" with Gabe.
Shop the Outlets with Jan.	Ice skate with Oscar.

Extracurriculars

Write the letter that matches the correct extracurricular activity to the right character.

1. _____	Michael	a.	yoga
2. _____	Phyllis	b.	community theatre
3. _____	Pam	c.	magic camp
4. _____	Dwight	d.	volleyball
5. _____	Jim	e.	bicycling
6. _____	Andy	f.	softball
7. _____	Toby	g.	bowling
8. _____	Darryl	h.	music
9. _____	Kevin	i.	writing
10. _____	Oscar	j.	karate

Match the Middle Name

Write the letter that matches the middle name to the correct first name.
What out for the trick one!

1. _____	Kelly	a.	Rajani Ghana
2. _____	Andy	b.	Bailey
3. _____	Pam	c.	Susan
4. _____	Erin	d.	Baines
5. _____	Ryan	e.	Kurt
6. _____	Gabe	f.	Gary
7. _____	Dwight	g.	Erin
8. _____	Michael	h.	Noelle
9. _____	Angela	i.	Morgan

Brother From Another Mother

Write the letter of the correct match next to the name of the characters sibling.

1.	_____	Michael	a. Rachel
2.	_____	Dwight	b. Walter
3.	_____	Darryl	c. Reed
4.	_____	Toby	d. Tom
5.	_____	Erin	e. Tiffany
6.	_____	Jim	f. Kenny
7.	_____	Andy	g. Gwenyth
8.	_____	Kelly	h. Fannie
9.	_____	Roy	i. Rory
10.	_____	Angela	j. a fake brother who steals your jeans

Their Other Jobs

Write the letter of the correct match next to the name of the characters other jobs or workplaces. Some may have had more than one other job. Others may have had the same job, so be careful!

1.	_____	Ryan	a. Osprey Paper
2.	_____	Danny	b. beauty pageant contestant
3.	_____	Daryll	c. Staples
4.	_____	Angela	d. bowling alley
5.	_____	Josh	e. drummer in a cover band
6.	_____	Jan	f. Athlead
7.	_____	Kevin	g. Staples
8.	_____	Michael	h. Taco Bell Express
9.	_____	Dwight	i. bar owner
10.	_____	Dwight	j. Scranton White Pages
11.	_____	Erin	k. fake ID business owner
12.	_____	Creed	l. bed and breakfast owner
13.	_____	Kevin	m. Men's Warehouse
14.	_____	Roy	n. bar owner
15.	_____	Danny	o. gravel company owner

Name that Dundie Winner

Write the letter of the correct match next to the name of the award winner.

_____	Kevin	a. Moving On Up Award
_____	Pam	b. Worst Salesman of the Year
_____	Dwight	c. Tight-Ass Award
_____	Oscar	d. Hottest in the Office (Multiple Years)
_____	Stanley	e. Bushiest Beaver Award
_____	Ryan	f. Promising Assistant Manager Award
_____	Daryll	g. Whitest Sneakers Award
_____	Kelly	h. Diabetes Award
_____	Phyllis	i. Doobie Doobie Pothead Stoner of the Year Award
_____	Toby	j. Extreme Repulsiveness Award
_____	Andy	k. Spicy Curry Award
_____	Angela	l. Don't Go in There After Me Award
_____	Jim	m. Best Dad Award

Match the Ex

Write the letter of the correct match next to the name who they used to date.

1. _____	Pam	a.	Jessica
2. _____	Jim	b.	Kathy
3. _____	Kelly	c.	Kelly
4. _____	Darryl	d.	Robert Lipton
5. _____	Andy	e.	Val
6. _____	Oscar	f.	Gabe
7. _____	Michael	g.	Stacy
8. _____	Holly	h.	Katie
9. _____	Kevin	i.	Donna
10. _____	Toby	j.	Darryl
11. _____	Stanley	k.	Gil
12. _____	Ryan	l.	Cynthia
13. _____	Angela	m.	Roy
14. _____	Erin	n.	AJ

Match the Ailment

Write the letter of the correct illness or ailment to the corresponding character.

1. _____ Meredith   a. Used to be in an iron lung

2. _____ Andy   b. Cooked Foot

3. _____ Darryl   c. Scoliosis

4. _____ DeAngelo   d. Kidney stones

5. _____ Meredith   e. Rabies

6. _____ Phylis   f. Irritable Bowel Syndrome

7. _____ Creed   g. Anal Fissures

8. _____ Michael   h. High blood pressure

9. _____ Angela   i. Dermatitis

10. _____ Kevin   j. Soy Allergy

11. _____ Jim   k. Dairy Allergy

12. _____ Dwight   l. Peanut Allergy

Name The Nickname

Write the letter of the correct nickname to the corresponding character.

1. ____	Gabe	a.	C-Span
2. ____	Stanley	b.	Nard Dog
3. ____	Phyllis	c.	Big Pregs
4. ____	Michael	d.	Stankley
5. ____	Pam	e.	Mr. Rogers
6. ____	Ryan	f.	Little Kevin
7. ____	Daryll	g.	Rye-Bread
8. ____	Oscar	h.	Birdman
9. ____	Andy	i.	Caleb Crawdad
10. ____	Dwight	j.	Monkey
11. ____	Jim	k.	Hillary Rodham Clinton
12. ____	Philip	l.	Possum
13. ____	Jan	m.	Mother Goose
14. ____	Angela	n.	Tuna

Halloween Costume Mix-Up

Who dressed up as what? Match the letter with the person who wore that Halloween costume!

1. _____	Pam	a.	Just Dracula (not Blackula)
2. _____	Erin	b.	Nancy Reagan
3. _____	Toby	c.	Uncle Sam
4. _____	Dwight	d.	Jesse Pinkman
5. _____	Oscar	e.	Lady Gaga
6. _____	Ryan	f.	Dr. Cinderella
7. _____	Creed	g.	OJ Simpson
8. _____	Darryl	h.	Snookie
9. _____	Kelly	i.	Osama Bin Laden
10. _____	Gabe	j.	Hugh Hefner
11. _____	Michael	k.	Sith Lord (not a monk)
12. _____	Angela	l.	Wendy from Wendy's

Whose Kid?

Write the letter of the correct match next to the name of their child

1. _____	Cece	a.	David Wallace
2. _____	Teddy	b.	Robert California
3. _____	Sasha	c.	Meredith
4. _____	Drake	d.	Jim and Pam
5. _____	Jake	e.	Toby
6. _____	Philip L.	f.	Dwight
7. _____	Bert	g.	Jan
8. _____	Jada	h.	Daryll
9. _____	Melissa	i.	Ryan
10. _____	Astrid	j.	Stanley

This or That #3

Circle your choice:

THIS	THAT
Bowling Alley Ryan	Corporate Ryan
Crentist the Dentist	The best tentist on the East Coast
cookies	brownies
Getting your uterus removed	Getting three vasectomies (snip snap, snip snap...)
Athlead	Athleap
Count Choculitus	Spontaneous Dento-Hydroplosion
Prison Mike	Date Mike
Milk and sugar	Scotch and Splenda
rabies	pelvical fracture
Who Would You Do	Desert Island

"The eyes are the groin of the face."

Creed's Crossword

ːross

2. _____ Charles Schneider
6. You have more fun as a follower, but you make more _____ as a leader.
8. I've been involved in a number of _____, both as a leader and a follower.
9. quabity assuance, but to a normal person
10. name of Creed's blog
12. smells like death

Down

1. pattern of thievery
3. band name
4. soup kitchen's featured item on Thursdays that Creed donates his Casino money to
5. Creed claims to have been treated with one of these as a child
7. what Creed sells out of the trunk of his car to young people
11. Hey, did one of you tell Stanley I have asthma? Because I don't, and if it gets out, they won't let me _____.

"I'm an early bird and I'm a night owl, so I'm wise and have worms."

Clark and Pete's Crossword

:ross

2. Clark brings back an espresso maker from this Campania Region holiday destination from his travels with Jan.

4. Jan ensures Clark has one of this before taking him abroad.

5. Pete's in-office love interest

8. they both grow a mustache with Toby for this

10. Andy hires this ex-girlfriend, to get back at Pete

12. Clark's nickname, not 'Fart'

13. Clark act like a creep and convinces Erin to audition for this role

Down

1. Clark's large inner ears make him particularly adept at this activity

3. Both are hired as _____ _____ representatives when Kelly and Ryan move to Ohio.

6. Pete's nickname

7. When Dwight and Clark pretend to be father and son, Dwight accuses Clark of being this type of collector.

9. movie that Pete knows, line for line

11. Pete is a native of this maple place

"I don't care what they say about me, I just wanna eat. Which I realize is a lot to ask for. At a dinner party."

Darryl's Crossword

cross

4. he breaks this container after this interview with Athlead, resulting in the death of the contents
6. 'Look, just be straight with me, man. You can be _____ with Matt, just be straight with me.'
9. Darryl sells this doll to Toby for $400
11. He works as the _____ of the warehouse.
12. Michael's practical joke ends with him falling and busting this body part

Down

1. shared religion with Pam
2. Michael whips out his negotiation techniques when Darryl asks for a modest raise of _____ _____.
3. ex-girlfriend, 'access your uncrazy side'
5. Darryl develops an allergy to this, which he says is in everything
7. material of the gloves that Darryl intends for Val, but diverts to Nate
8. 'What'd I tell you about building forts in my _____'
10. Daughter's name

"That is sort of an oaky afterbirth."

One Liners Crossword

Across

4. Well, happy birthday, _____. Sorry your party's so lame.

6. If you pray enough, you can change yourself into a _____ _____.

8. Steer clear Big Tuna. Head for _____ _____.

11. I'm forced to go to the American Girl store and order clothes for large _____ _____.

13. You can't fire me, I don't work in this ___!

14. 'Hi, I'm date Mike. Nice to _____ _____'

Down

1. I am one of the few people who looks hot eating a _____.

2. Sorry I annoyed you with my _____.

3. The trick is to _____ the onions.

5. I'm not superstitious, but I am a little _____.

7. Crazy world, lotta _____.

9. Monkey see, monkey do. Monkey _____ _____ _____ you.

10. I want to be wined, dined, and _____-_____.

12. Gum's gotten _____ lately. Have you noticed?

"Did I stutter?"

Stanley Hudson's Crossword

ross

3. Michael's nickname for Stanley
4. What he would rather be doing than working
5. A day Stanley likes
8. A movement Stanley was involved in when he was eating whatever he wanted'
9. Stanley would like a decommissioned one to live in
10. Who do you want on your Florida team?

Down

1. Alerts Stanley when his stress goes up
2. A doubled up kitchen appliance
5. Stanley once got a Dundie award for being the face of this debilitating disease
7. That person? That woman is not my mother. She is my step mother.'

"In the wild, there is no healthcare. In the wild healthcare is, 'Ow, I hurt my leg. I can't run. A lion eats me, and I'm dead.' Well, I'm not dead. I'm the lion. You're dead."

The Injury Crossword

ross

. celestial body, body part

. breakfast meat of the buttled

. superior quality of the Prism Duro-Sport

. elbow plus wall bump equals a

0. actor with the rare disability of growing into a man vernight

1. country of origin of the website that sells cheap songs

3. town where the gas station was yamless

Down

1. other superior quality of the Prism Duro-Sport

3. sweet medium in which to hide crushed aspirin

4. Michael's margarine of preference

5. more serious than a foot injury

6. breakroom snack, just go for it

9. word Dwight is seen typing over and over

12. I wanna clamp Michael's _____ in a George Foreman grill.

"If I had a gun with two bullets and I was in a room with Hitler, Bin Laden and Toby, I would shoot Toby twice."

General Knowledge Crossword

oss

Kevin's magic number
Kevin and Creed's Halloween costume
the worst thing about prison
Oscar's dogs name
Who Michael thinks he sees in NYC
. This person let Dwight steer the boar
. Bob Vance, Vance _____.
. What Michael wants in his scotch

Down

1. has been paid $150,000 over 20 years by Dwight for a hobby
2. Andy's alma mater
3. social group where no paper, plastic, or work talk is allowed
7. owns a dog named Ruby, who may be dead

"People underestimate the power of nostalgia. Nostalgia is truly one of the greatest human weaknesses, second only to the neck."

Schrute Farms

2. co-owner of the farm
6. This website is the lifeblood of the agritourism industry
8. themed room, water
10. themed room, country
12. the most attractive beets
13. the farmhouse has nine of these
14. themed room, dark

Down
1. rich in folate, this crop is grown on Dwight's Farm
3. original acreage
4. who Angela actually marries here
5. where Dwight's farmhouse bathroom is located
7. era in which the Battle of Schrute Farms was fought
9. 'So what kind of farming you into, huh? You more of a fruit man or a _____ _____?'
11. who Angela plans to marry here

"My, philosophy is, basically this. And this is something that I live by. And I always have. And I always will. Don't, ever, for any reason, do anything, to anyone, for any reason, ever, no matter what, no matter where, or who you are with, or, or where you are going, or, or where you've been. Ever. For any reason. Whatsoever."

The Party Planning Committee

Across

4. Baby Shower M&Ms-girl name
5. Historic person who attend's Phyllis' Bridal Shower
6. This person blackmailed her way to become head of the committee
7. Themes of the rival Christmas party thrown by Karen and Pam
8. To celebrate Dunder Mifflin Infinity, not a midday meal
11. bad dessert choice for Meredith's surprise party, given her dairy allergy

Down

1. Happens only once every billion years
2. Theme of the party that featured hummus plates, pita triangles
3. Baby Shower M&Ms-boy name
9. Welcome party for this person was bad on purpose, carrot cake, magician
10. Eventually shut down by this character

"Jim said mixed berries? Oh wow... Yeah, he's on to me."

Jim and Pam Crossword

cross
4. honeymoon inside joke, other couple
6. state of marriage
7. what cartoon jim becomes, post radioactive bear bite
8. Jim purchased these at Toby's party before Andy swooped in
9. type of flooring in Jim's parent's house
10. vessel of inside jokes, love
11. favorite yogurt of half the couple
13. location of proposal
14. honeymoon location

Down
1. Angela's game, played between Jim and Pam's desk
2. once a spiritual experience, now kitschy; place.
3. vessel of love, boat
5. little ladybug Halpert
12. Named after grandfather (or favorite cat)

"Hey Goldenface! Go puck yourself!"

Help Find Michael's Moppy Place

When arrogant salesmen are mean to my face, a certain manager will go to his moppy place.

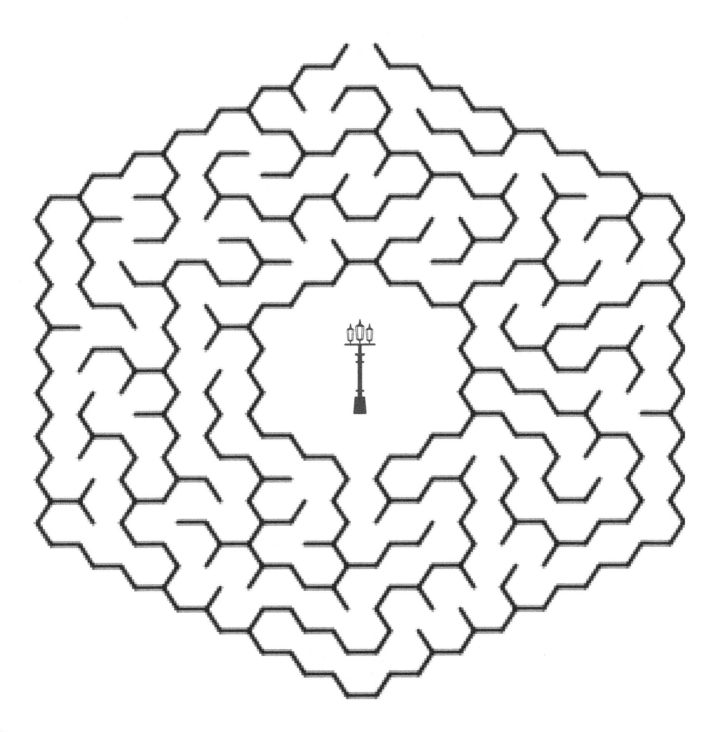

He means his mopey place, it's under that streetlamp that he thinks was in Casablanca

Help Erin Find Her Birth Parents

But not like "hate" hate. More just like, "Mom, I hate you!" And then she would say "go to your room, young lady." And I'd stamp my foot and run upstairs and I have a room, which is really cool. And then we'd just have dinner together. But I don't know. I'd have to meet her.

"I'm probably just another Porky's baby."

Help Kevin Find His Toupee

"It's not a good idea. There's no such thing as a good hairpiece."

"Yeah. But that's easy enough for you to say, Oscar. You have that thick, beautiful, Chicano hair. So nice."

Help Phyllis Finish Her Mittens

Phyllis, are my mittens done?

"It's almost done, but you can't get them wet, and they can't be dry-cleaned either. You have to hand wash without water, wring-dry gently, and use a hairdryer on cool."

Help Andy Become the A Capela Star of his Dreams

"Because I was a freaking rock star in college. When I joined Here Comes Treble, that's when I became somebody."

"The more I hear about all this a capella drama, the more I think it's kind of pathetic. But when you're with someone, you put up with the stuff that makes you lose respect for them, and that is love."

Help Meredith Find her PhD

"Um, for the first seven years, I was getting my PhD in School Psychology and they didn't show it."

"Yes, I was getting hammered but, hey, it was college."

Help Roy Find His True, Non-Pam Love

"It was a year ago today that I met Laura...You are full of surprises. You are my beautiful mystery girl."

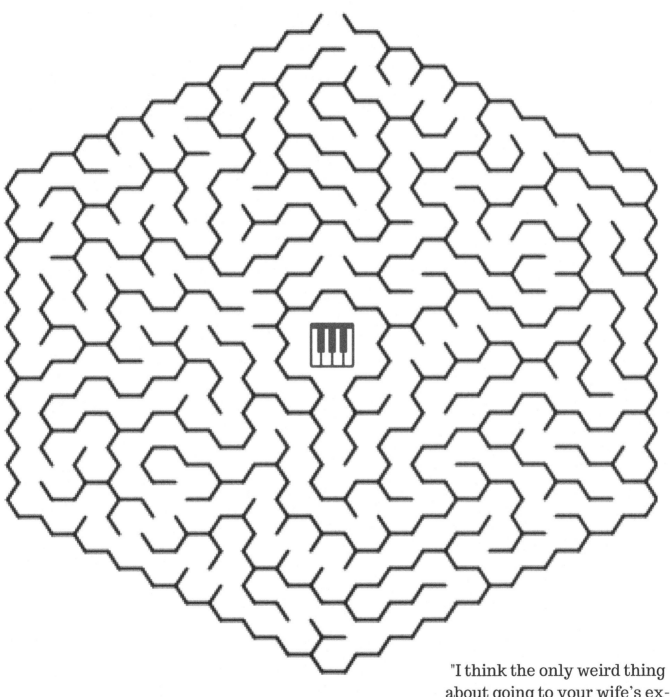

"I think the only weird thing about going to your wife's ex-fiancé's wedding on a weekday at eight AM is that it's your wife's ex-fiancé."

Jan Levinson, I presume?

You know Pam, in Spain, they often don't even start eating until midnight.

```
F  X  S  C  H  I  N  E  S  E  F  O  O  D  D  V  F  L  D  T
Q  W  P  K  U  Q  Y  D  S  W  I  A  R  P  I  Y  R  F  N  Q
H  D  S  G  T  Y  U  B  I  Z  I  I  C  F  E  M  W  E  V  G
P  O  H  R  N  B  O  Z  L  I  Q  X  I  F  S  W  M  D  F  J
W  N  W  O  S  W  D  I  I  K  R  L  T  K  N  E  Y  I  N  O
R  A  F  C  E  I  F  I  H  C  N  A  Q  G  C  X  X  L  K  G
E  J  O  U  I  T  T  J  C  C  I  F  J  N  O  V  Z  P  F  V
W  Y  L  B  L  T  H  D  E  Y  A  M  A  Y  K  U  H  F  U  F
W  B  I  O  P  Z  A  P  I  V  V  H  M  V  I  U  L  K  A  O
D  Y  A  S  P  D  B  A  Z  R  N  T  A  B  U  T  X  D  C  P
Q  T  G  S  U  F  M  P  N  E  T  U  I  A  C  I  B  V  U  L
V  I  E  O  S  J  D  K  B  O  Q  S  C  V  B  U  B  F  D  I
A  N  F  E  L  H  E  O  J  X  S  L  A  H  U  N  T  E  R  L
T  E  G  H  A  R  O  S  T  R  O  L  Y  A  T  E  N  N  A  Y
Y  R  Z  K  T  B  U  O  F  I  C  S  K  L  I  Q  L  D  C  E
M  E  B  N  I  C  X  W  G  Z  O  W  D  Z  Z  M  C  L  J  D
D  S  H  R  P  N  E  E  U  Q  E  C  I  N  B  B  B  Y  P  Q  H
E  Q  G  B  S  D  U  F  N  F  R  K  J  Q  Z  W  X  G  Y  T
U  M  C  G  O  D  Z  I  L  L  A  R  Y  Q  V  J  Y  Z  N  Z
O  Q  S  F  H  C  Q  Z  I  B  X  N  V  B  P  Y  G  C  X  P
```

SERENITY BY JAN   HUNTER   GOULD
FOLIAGE   ANNE TAYLOR   CHILI'S
JAMAICA   CHINESE FOOD   ASTRID
HOSPITAL SUPPLIES   OSSO BUCO   BOOB ENHANCEMENT
GODZILLARY   ICE QUEEN

Toby

Why are you the way that you are?

```
V  V  X  U  K  P  G  D  E  P  R  N  P  V  N  L  J  N  P  H
Y  P  A  A  F  G  J  I  M  I  N  L  Y  Y  J  K  H  R  B  H
K  D  I  N  D  Y  E  Q  A  I  V  J  P  U  K  M  O  O  C  Y
P  V  Z  A  U  F  W  H  M  E  S  E  R  P  A  C  N  C  N  L
G  X  I  G  N  O  Y  K  U  C  H  Y  Y  S  V  F  N  I  R  A
G  G  P  P  D  J  B  S  H  Z  D  C  X  T  Q  Z  K  N  V  Z
X  S  L  H  E  M  O  H  V  U  Y  H  F  G  T  C  U  L  N
K  G  I  R  R  H  U  B  T  F  R  A  D  S  L  S  A  S  H  A
M  D  N  Z  B  M  B  Y  L  Q  O  D  I  S  X  S  U  S  L  E
Z  P  E  X  A  W  R  R  I  Z  R  F  Q  T  T  E  D  E  N  M
R  T  J  K  L  X  C  R  A  Y  W  L  W  R  K  M  I  C  O  B
V  S  N  N  L  M  S  O  N  B  X  E  W  A  K  X  V  N  S  T
X  M  C  R  X  P  E  R  S  O  G  N  F  N  X  I  O  I  D  G
P  X  F  E  W  O  M  D  L  T  A  D  T  G  Z  Y  R  R  C  L
I  H  V  B  S  D  I  J  I  Y  A  E  L  L  N  Y  C  P  Z  S
G  S  P  M  U  J  N  T  V  X  Y  R  G  E  O  C  E  K  G  U
L  D  I  E  T  C  A  J  E  E  B  M  I  R  B  W  D  D  L  H
S  R  T  V  P  G  R  E  X  S  V  A  Y  C  I  O  Q  W  E  L
F  T  S  O  K  D  Y  P  X  H  W  N  M  O  A  E  E  N  H  M
H  Q  N  M  V  I  G  N  A  F  N  L  A  Y  M  D  N  E  F  M
```

PRINCESS UNICORN	COSTA RICA	EVIL SNAIL
ZIPLINE	STRANGLER	MOVEMBER
HR	JURY DUTY	CHAD FLENDERMAN
DUNDERBALL	SASHA	SEMINARY
DIVORCED	CAPRESE	SEXY TOBY

The Cats of Angela Martin

Those lumps are cats, and those cats have names.

```
M F R O Y D J Y W U W Q I L S D N H J J
V G B A N D I T T W O V M H X L E U A A
V F W F B P A W L I C K B A G G I N S I
W R L P R I N C E S S L A D Y J B Q M N
F K U Y U J L Y L S E S C A K T Z Q A T
C R M A M O E A U H U E P C R I R Q A S
O D P Y W O T P A G I P O M T N A T D Y
L G Y U T E E G H Y C T O K L K R G U Y
T D A B P L S H W I S F Y R H I L F Z Y
O R N A K H A T X M L L W T Z E T A Y M
V J K N F D X D O Q C I D T X E D X U A
Y W I D Y N M C Y D S A P M N N U R Q V
A R D I D X I N A A P I C S H Q Y B D K
C E V T L L L X H L R M N Q E O M D I I
X L H A N J K O E F I A J M R A S H A C
D Q X F E W Y V M F N F G V K Z T W N Y
P L J F C J X V W K X U O C M A P E X
D A G A R B A G E D L L Q K R H J J E U
J D E B Z K Y E U Z E X O K C N A Z U I
D B H R V D U D S S S H Z E M B E R U T
```

SPRINKLES	GARBAGE	BANDIT
PRINCESS LADY	MR. ASH	PETALS
COMSTOCK	EMBER	MILKYWAY
DIANE	LUMPY	PHILIP
TINKIE	CRINKLEPUSS	BANDIT TWO
PAWLICK BAGGINS	LADY ARAGORN	

The Warehouse

Managing the warehouse is a very important part of my job. And I haven't been there in months.

```
F  M  Y  H  Y  R  R  E  J  A  H  D  B  L  J  V  D  L  A  O
O  O  K  R  H  G  B  C  V  W  L  E  O  N  Y  G  V  L  Y  J
C  X  E  M  J  A  L  H  E  G  T  N  N  E  L  G  I  A  W  Q
U  S  L  A  V  R  O  Z  L  A  N  E  O  C  Q  D  A  M  S  S
A  H  F  B  P  D  V  Q  N  Y  F  K  Y  P  H  I  T  W  F  I
T  X  Q  W  K  Y  E  I  F  Q  B  J  F  O  M  O  M  R  C  P
F  P  U  B  Z  Y  R  D  X  D  M  R  T  H  S  R  O  I  G  R
C  I  B  U  S  N  R  P  Y  I  A  F  T  Y  K  U  J  H  R  Q
A  Y  U  F  R  A  D  H  C  N  Q  C  E  I  A  V  M  K  Z  Z
W  H  O  D  U  O  Y  H  K  P  G  R  X  A  D  L  U  I  R  N
S  J  P  O  Z  H  A  K  I  N  Z  H  R  B  M  L  M  P  C  Q
P  D  I  A  O  E  J  Q  U  D  H  C  W  J  M  M  K  R  V  Z
E  C  L  C  L  J  G  M  D  J  E  L  W  Q  S  E  E  H  J  M
Q  E  I  U  H  C  D  D  Q  M  Y  I  F  B  V  I  B  K  W  G
N  P  H  V  E  G  D  B  A  R  F  X  O  Y  V  D  E  M  I  A
K  U  P  D  X  O  M  N  R  M  O  S  G  Q  H  B  V  C  E  N
L  B  X  H  S  H  J  A  S  S  L  Y  T  F  Q  I  V  Q  L  E
T  Q  D  C  U  T  D  X  T  Z  W  X  E  O  Z  C  P  F  Y  W
V  U  G  F  Q  Z  W  B  F  T  S  V  Z  J  Y  Q  C  M  O  V
K  O  L  U  G  G  X  N  W  A  L  E  D  D  P  S  W  H  B  P
```

ROY	HIDE	LONNY
DARRYL	FRANK	GLENN
MICHAEL	MADGE	NATE
PHILIP	VAL	JERRY
MATT		

The Works

Michael: Is there anyway that you could do all, all of them?
Pretzel guy: The Works. You got it.

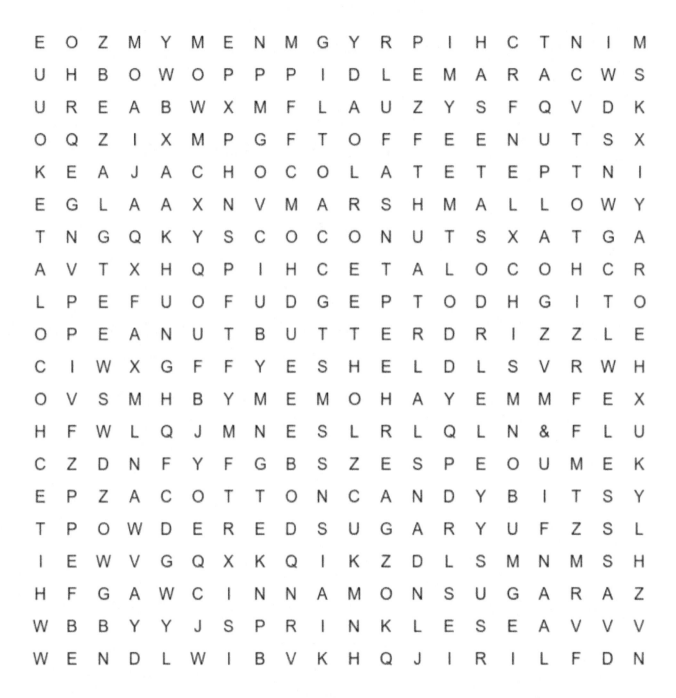

E O Z M Y M E N M G Y R P I H C T N I M
U H B O W O P P P I D L E M A R A C W S
U R E A B W X M F L A U Z Y S F Q V D K
O Q Z I X M P G F T O F F E E N U T S X
K E A J A C H O C O L A T E T E P T N I
E G L A A X N V M A R S H M A L L O W Y
T N G Q K Y S C O C O N U T S X A T G A
A V T X H Q P I H C E T A L O C O H C R
L P E F U O F U D G E P T O D H G I T O
O P E A N U T B U T T E R D R I Z Z L E
C I W X G F F Y E S H E L D L S V R W H
O V S M H B Y M E M O H A Y E M M F E X
H F W L Q J M N E S L R L Q L N & F L U
C Z D N F Y F G B S Z E S P E O U M E K
E P Z A C O T T O N C A N D Y B I T S Y
T P O W D E R E D S U G A R Y U F Z S L
I E W V G Q X K Q I K Z D L S M N M S H
H F G A W C I N N A M O N S U G A R A Z
W B B Y Y J S P R I N K L E S E A V V V
W E N D L W I B V K H Q J I R I L F D N

SWEET GLAZE	CINNAMON SUGAR	CHOCOLATE
WHITE CHOCOLATE	FUDGE	M&MS
CARAMEL DIP	MINT CHIP	CHOCOLATE CHIP
MARSHMALLOW	NUTS	TOFFEE NUTS
COCONUTS	PEANUT BUTTER DRIZZLE	OREOS
SPRINKLES	COTTON CANDY BITS	POWDERED SUGAR

Meredith

You should stay. I have Vienna sausages...and napkins.

```
W  S  A  J  V  J  L  C  B  X  S  S  E  I  B  A  R  O  Z  L
X  Z  S  V  F  Q  W  Y  D  K  D  F  F  F  N  R  C  U  N  L
H  S  C  H  O  O  L  P  S  Y  C  H  O  L  O  G  Y  T  A  O
I  E  Q  R  W  F  U  X  F  S  J  K  U  N  S  K  A  B  P  R
R  I  A  X  O  U  G  X  I  G  Z  C  K  A  Q  G  Y  A  R  K
E  S  G  D  U  F  Z  F  G  Y  W  R  I  Y  D  M  W  C  I  O
E  Y  N  E  L  T  N  R  G  O  H  N  E  G  O  B  V  K  U  B
D  G  I  Q  Z  I  D  F  U  P  B  I  E  T  M  G  M  S  A  Z
N  R  C  E  V  V  C  X  R  A  A  N  C  G  E  X  N  T  P  N
U  E  N  T  A  B  G  E  H  I  I  E  C  Z  G  X  B  E  M  F
D  L  A  L  E  B  T  E  C  T  R  K  W  N  Y  I  T  A  K  O
M  L  D  A  T  Q  R  R  A  E  P  H  H  X  T  F  X  K  E  J
O  A  Y  N  E  H  K  L  T  M  K  E  D  E  Y  Z  A  H  S  J
M  Y  L  X  Z  S  H  S  Y  W  Q  O  M  W  V  O  Q  O  W  M
T  R  L  C  J  E  Y  X  F  E  K  W  H  G  C  D  M  U  V  H
S  I  E  H  R  H  N  O  S  R  E  P  P  I  R  T  S  S  D  R
E  A  B  P  J  H  H  S  L  U  O  U  X  G  W  E  P  E  Y  R
B  D  E  S  U  P  P  L  I  E  R  R  E  L  A  T  I  O  N  S
M  S  Y  A  D  S  K  C  I  R  T  A  P  T  S  I  R  O  C  B
C  F  K  C  K  C  M  I  N  I  V  A  N  Z  D  Q  I  T  Y  X
```

SUPPLIER RELATIONS   DAIRY ALLERGY   BELLYDANCING
RABIES   STRIPPER SON   BAT BITE
MINIVAN   HYSTERECTOMY   ST. PATRICK'S DAY
REHAB   OUTBACK STEAKHOUSE   BEST MOM DUNDEE
GENITAL HERPES   SCHOOL PSYCHOLOGY   HEAD LICE

Threat Level Midnight

It'll take a lot more than a bullet to the brain, lungs, heart, back and balls to kill
Michael Scarn!

```
Z  C  W  X  V  D  M  O  P  T  H  E  I  C  E  O  J  S  X  Q
T  B  U  C  X  N  U  X  H  K  U  Y  H  H  W  R  I  O  L  F
H  R  X  B  D  P  X  J  G  Y  M  Q  W  Q  O  F  R  M  Y  S
E  T  T  K  I  T  E  S  I  G  J  R  R  L  I  K  U  U  M  Y
S  S  M  U  A  H  A  U  K  R  E  L  T  U  B  T  O  B  O  R
C  F  Q  W  C  S  F  C  L  C  R  I  Y  H  U  F  R  A  T  U
A  G  H  K  H  Q  Y  W  Y  E  A  U  H  C  V  H  A  A  K  E
R  W  T  C  Y  I  N  B  U  K  S  J  C  X  X  P  L  O  O  I
N  F  K  L  B  I  J  M  N  L  N  M  E  P  T  U  L  V  X  Q
G  Y  N  F  V  A  Q  Q  B  O  N  U  I  E  G  S  S  S  L  P
O  D  N  S  M  N  Q  S  H  U  W  A  F  V  K  G  T  F  K  M
S  Y  E  C  A  F  N  E  D  L  O  G  O  P  P  O  A  W  C  X
C  E  Q  R  H  N  M  R  U  K  R  M  Y  G  N  E  R  J  Y  I
V  H  Z  E  A  I  J  Z  Q  V  C  E  K  J  X  M  G  E  Z  G
E  U  O  E  G  V  F  N  J  O  K  M  F  L  L  O  A  H  H  T
B  U  K  N  L  V  Q  U  N  C  P  J  S  G  J  T  M  X  D  C
E  I  C  P  Y  N  T  F  O  R  B  O  C  U  A  C  E  I  S  G
S  A  L  L  M  I  C  H  A  E  L  S  C  A  R  N  R  N  E  B
D  K  F  A  Q  G  J  K  Q  N  S  T  T  G  I  W  D  U  H  C
Y  K  E  Y  O  Z  U  N  R  Z  O  I  C  I  A  D  F  E  G  D
```

GOLDENFACE	MICHAEL SCARN	HOCKEY
DWIGT	ROBOT BUTLER	CHEROKEE JACK
SCREENPLAY	ALL STAR GAME	FBI
THE SCARN	FUNKY CAT	MOP THE ICE

Cameos

Find the names of the various celebrity cameos who can be seen in the Office over the years. Can you remember them all?

```
F  M  E  Q  T  A  K  J  Q  E  L  O  V  T  N  P  R  N  K  V
M  W  V  K  N  A  B  O  R  G  H  S  O  J  C  E  M  V  Q  S
P  I  C  C  M  Y  K  C  X  I  U  A  U  A  T  Q  T  F  T  G
E  L  F  A  T  E  Z  C  Z  C  M  A  H  A  I  T  D  E  B  A
A  L  H  L  E  R  X  M  X  E  R  K  L  Z  E  I  P  R  F  D
U  F  X  B  F  R  D  V  S  K  B  S  H  N  E  H  H  A  J  O
G  E  N  K  F  A  J  F  K  T  N  E  R  K  E  I  M  Y  X  U
Z  R  F  C  U  C  F  C  X  A  B  A  B  N  V  M  J  R  F  C
Q  R  M  A  B  M  K  J  I  Y  L  V  C  N  A  H  B  O  I  S
W  E  F  J  N  I  A  T  G  L  X  O  N  B  G  V  D  M  G  U
D  L  J  B  E  J  S  L  I  D  L  L  Q  A  J  U  A  O  P
S  L  O  P  R  I  B  W  B  B  P  A  E  M  L  R  B  N  Q  C
M  C  A  X  R  Z  N  O  E  Z  A  J  T  C  D  H  D  O  R  M
A  B  N  H  A  Z  G  R  I  C  K  Y  G  E  R  V  A  I  S  L
D  E  C  T  W  S  T  Y  I  A  B  L  E  S  I  R  D  I  E  C
A  X  U  B  Q  L  E  S  B  X  C  E  L  J  Q  E  H  P  E  U
Y  G  S  F  S  L  S  Y  D  Q  J  B  C  W  L  M  V  C  D  R
M  X  A  M  A  E  A  U  G  H  V  Y  J  Z  X  N  M  K  T  O
A  O  C  W  J  T  R  S  E  T  A  B  Y  H  T  A  K  W  S  B
N  S  K  B  Z  W  L  P  C  K  E  P  W  O  U  I  P  E  O  Z
```

IDRIS ELBA	STEPHEN COLBERT	JOAN CUSACK
WARREN BUFFET	RAY ROMANO	WILL FERRELL
JIM CARREY	AMY ADAMS	JOSH GROBAN
JACK BLACK	JESSICA ALBA	RICKY GERVAIS
WILL ARNETT	CHRISTIAN SLATER	KATHY BATES

The Scranton Strangler

"Thank you Scranton Strangler. I love you. You just took one more person's breath away!"

```
T N E M H S I N U P L A T I P A C L Q B
P O Z D I B M A Q C S F Q N H L L Q F Z
K S U H J E M Y I Y H A L L O W E E N O
E I I S A N G E R W Y P C A T J U O B C
J R V G M X O S N P B Z B Y S Z E E U G
Q P A M I C X Q K G H B W U G T X H Q W
V O C A L C H O R D S M I P L N F A S F
P R P W Y A D H T R I B S E C E C K D L
L S K X G C C R J O M Z T S O C T E R K
C A Z D H A R B N B J D O U V O P V A G
S N F X P R X S L S E R P X Y N U O W N
F U F U I C Z T T C A M O O T N E Z O M
O L B V P H Z R R L D O T F U I R Y H E
Z E E M P A N A D A S E T I D U N G E J
K C Z A K S H N M R F P Y Q Y B E C G N
X I Z D S E M G B E A B T R R K S H R M
T L O J F Y T L T G C M L J U U T O O X
W O X R E S N E C K S K I V J W O J E N
I P I M W O R O R I J K U H Z J S R G F
H U S D K D S G Q Q K B G X R L P K H A
```

GEORGE HOWARD SKUB   JURY DUTY   CECE'S BIRTHDAY
HALLOWEEN   EMPANADAS   ERNESTO'S
PRISON   NECK   ANGER
GUILTY   INNOCENT   STRANGLE
CAR CHASE   POLICE   CAPITAL PUNISHMENT
VOCAL CHORDS

Break Me Off A Piece of That...

Gimme a break, gimme a break, break me off a piece of that... I am totally blanking. What is the thing?

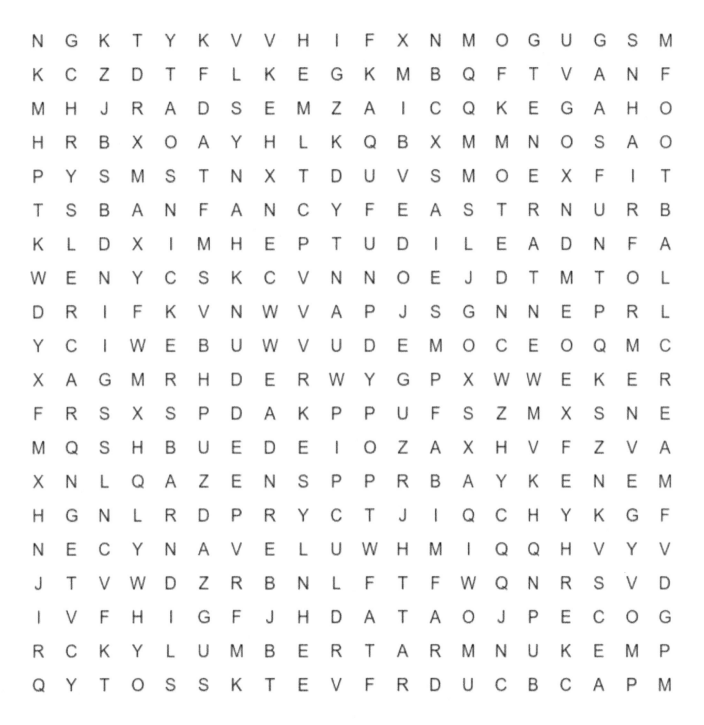

N G K T Y K V V H I F X N M O G U G S M
K C Z D T F L K E G K M B Q F T V A N F
M H J R A D S E M Z A I C Q K E G A H O
H R B X O A Y H L K Q B X M M N O S A O
P Y S M S T N X T D U V S M O E X F I T
T S B A N F A N C Y F E A S T R N U R B
K L D X I M H E P T U D I L E A D N F A
W E N Y C S K C V N N O E J D T M T O L
D R I F K V N W V A P J S G N N E P R L
Y C I W E B U W V U D E M O C E O Q M C
X A G M R H D E R W Y G P X W W E K E R
F R S X S P D A K P P U F S Z M X S N E
M Q S H B U E D E I O Z A X H V F Z V A
X N L Q A Z E N S P P R B A Y K E N E M
H G N L R D P R Y C T J I Q C H Y K G F
N E C Y N A V E L U W H M I Q Q H V Y V
J T V W D Z R B N L F T F W Q N R S V D
I V F H I G F J H D A T A O J P E C O G
R C K Y L U M B E R T A R M N U K E M P
Q Y T O S S K T E V F R D U C B C A P M

CHRYSLER CAR   FOOTBALL CREAM   LUMBER TAR
SNICKERS BAR   GREY POUPON   CLAUDE VAN DAMME
HAIR FOR MEN   POISON GAS   NUTRASWEET
FANCY FEAST

Minor Characters

```
K E Z B Y Z Z U P D W P E N E R I W A A D G B F
K H G R A V H B T U T N Y Y F K H V J I C Q I U
E B D P E M R G O V I I Q H K I L W V R A Q C H
S T H E S C R A N T O N S T R A N G L E R H R F
P W B N W B C Q S G H Q A A G K U C I P P Q S Q
S M N M H Z J U T Y H P L C Y R X M N P F X K C
W M H N L O J V N G U W V L R L K O X I C O M E
O D I R T S A M A S Q F I S O Y H A N R S E O Z
Y P V Q K U P Q H E M M W N H A K J M T V J J O
T U W L W U O T C R A E T A N F H P X S K U X N
J C J G O K U D R F X T J K A A Q H C E Y G N I
D A J D J R N Q E R U W T M D A N S W H X U L G
Z J K J B R Q C M V W A B R I A N X D T V R N D
L W U E C D N M Y B T V R H P Z N H T H I H K N
I X A O P I F U L E G Q T D N K W O C T Q H I A
A R P I R A D F L O T N D W R G T K E E D V U O
V L V P S P L X I F Y B O B A D N E R B G I F E
X A E A C P A M B C D R J B S Q F N B A B V Y L
R H V B K C A C E O B D C H F C O H H Z Z Z Y M
T U Q G C R V S B R T G Z J A D D Z X I X F B U
N W N G K P R O M D K R X N Q Y Z S L Y S S P
Y W S I C U S Y I A I B N A T Q B E W E I I E A
C G V F N B F E L E V R R T U S H K T D K F D N
M M E E G B P Y E O H B Z B G B E R J T B F M S
```

BRIAN
HANK TATE
BRANDON
ASTRID
BRENDA
LEO AND GINO

JUSTINE
MR. BROWN
ELIZABETH THE STRIPPER
JAKE PALMER
BILLY MERCHANT
IRENE

THE SCRANTON STRANGLER
THE PRINCE FAMILY
VIKRAM
NURSE CYNTHIA
RAVI
CATHY

The Regulars

```
J E H G Q G V A I W U D Z Z J Q W L O L
T Y C R Z U S L P W G W D E E R C Q T W
O K A W L Y I Z Z C M H C H M K U F M D
W K J Q Q Y R V I X D F E L X T D H N
V I Q S E X G Y C O G D N U U O Q X J I
A Q X A Y M J H E A A A S I B I J J X R
D O S C A R A L M W K W Z Y J I M V R E
A K N I F E N P G C J P J J E M M L I H
R Q M Y L X T W E W Q X Q I D W I G H T
R X G Z L L H C Y Q B K Q X M L X R M M
Y G J W F L Y H X P A E B Z C W I A J M
L Y B Y C A E H W H H Q L N M L N J P D
E E C E T E H K P X M V M E G D Y T A L
T P K L N I C G X T U R E Y B I Z B B
W W Z N A N G E L A M E E Q I B E K N L
S D M A Y I L P P L D T C L K K G P M C
Y K A T R V I I F I O W B W N K R U H M
O Q P S E E K G T P Y O E D R O X C P F
G U W P T K Q H T W Z B P X Y T B J M R
S O Q Y O F F B O X B K M G Y A E Z E U
```

STANLEY	DWIGHT	MICHAEL
PAM	JIM	RYAN
ANDY	KEVIN	MEREDITH
ANGELA	OSCAR	PHYLLIS
ROY	JAN	KELLY
TOBY	CREED	DARRYL
ERIN		

The
Answers

Mini Quiz #1: Answers

1. What is not a pretzel day topping?
   D. butterscotch bits

2. What does Angela call her grandmother?
   C. Nana Mimi

3. Who is not an accountant?
   A. Creed

4. Where does Jan's sister live?
   D. Scottsdale

5. Who did Dwight play in the 7th grade production of "Oklahoma!"?
   E. Mutey the Mailman

6. What is the name of the exercise equipment Dwight sits on?
   E. fitness orb

7. Who wins the hot dog eating contest?
   A. Andy

Mini Quiz #2: Answers

1. What is the name of Kevin's ex-fiance?
   B. Stacy

2. What does Michael yell from the front of the Booze Cruise?
   D. I'm King of the World!

3. What is a nate-pon?
   A. Coupon from Nate for things like tickles and gum

4. Who is not a character in the murder mystery game?
   C. Min T. Julep

5. What is the worst part about prison?
   E. the dementors

6. What does Dwight find under the seat of Meredith's mini van?
   A. bottle of alcohol

7. Who went missing from Phyllis' wedding?
   B. Uncle Al

Mini Quiz #3: Answers

1. What is the most important thing to do when a new baby is born?
   D. mark it secretly in a kind of a mark that only you could recognize and no baby snatcher can ever copy

2. What vehicle served as Phyllis and Bob's wedding getaway car?
   B. A Vance Refridgeration Work Vehicle

3. What is not a way that Michael has come close to hurting himself?
   B. Firing a gun in the office

4. Who does not go to Pam's art show?
   A. Toby

5. What is not a text read by the Finer Things Club?
   A. Lolita

6. What is Gabe said to be afraid of?
   B. flying

7. Why was Dwight shunned by his family as a child?
   D. He failed to save the excess oil from a can of tuna

Mini Quiz #4: Answers

1. What was the movie that inspired Movie Mondays?
   A. Varsity Blues

2. What did Micheal sell at his telemarketing job?
   D. diet pills

3. Who has Kelly not kissed?
   C. Andy

4. What costume does Carol wear to Diwali?
   A. cheerleader

5. What romantic comedy does Kelly mention when she describes how Netflix works?
   B. Love Actually

6. What is not an ingredient in Michael's birthday subs?
   D. black olives

7. What is not one of the group names on Beach Day?
   A. Ryan's Team

Mini Quiz 5: Answers

1. How long were Ryan and Kelly married?
   C. a week

2. What state does Kelly move to that Ryan also decides to move to "for unrelated reasons"?
   D. Ohio

3. On the eve of what holiday do Kelly and Ryan first hook up?
   B. Valentine's Day

4. What did Ryan do at Dwight's wedding so he could talk to Kelly?
   A. give his baby an allergic reaction

5. What does the line "Kapoor and kadesperate" refer to?
   D. opening lines of a poem Ryan writes about Kelly

6. Why does Ryan call Kelly in the middle of the night?
   E. he thinks there is a murderer in his apartment

7. Why do Ryan and Kelly get divorced?
   C. Ryan says he doesn't want to be married until everyone can be married

Mini Quiz #6: Answers

1. Where was William Charles Snyder born?
   A. California

2. What does Kelly want to name her future baby?
   B. Usher Jennifer Hudson Kapoor

3. When Meredith contracts rabies, what is not an animal that has bitten her recently?
   C. squirrel

4. What does it say on Mose's shirt when he is about to wrestle Ryan in the barn?
   E. "Fear"

5. What is Michael's ringtone?
   B. My Humps

6. What two animals were seen engaging in an unspeakable act on the paper with the obscene watermark?
   A. duck + mouse

7. What is the name of Andy's part time frozen yogurt chef girlfriend?
   D. Jamie

Fill in the Blank #1: Answers

1. _____Poop_____ is raining from the ceilings. _____Poop!_____

2. I sprout _____mung_____ _____beans_____ on a damp paper towel in my desk drawer. Very nutritious. But they smell like _____death._____

3. It has to be official, and it has to be _____urine._____

4. Why tip someone for a job I'm capable of doing myself? I can deliver food. I can drive a taxi. I can, and do, cut my own _____hair._____ I did, however, tip my urologist, because... I am unable to _____pulverize_____ my own _____kidney_____ _____stones._____

5. Yes, it is true. I, _____Michael_____ _____Scott,_____ am signing up with an online dating service. Thousands of people have done it, and I am going to do it. I need a username. And... I have a great one. _____Little_____ _____kid_____ _____lover._____

6. _____Jim_____ is not allowed to talk until after he buys me a _____coke._____ Those are the rules of jinx, and they are unflinchingly rigid.

7. I wake up every morning in a bed that's too _____small,_____ drive my daughter to a school that's too _____expensive,_____ and then I go to work to a job for which I get _____paid_____ too little, but on _____Pretzel_____ Day? Well, I like _____pretzel_____ day.

8. Please don't throw _____garbage_____ at me.

9. I want the job. I really do. It's just, the rest of my family's in the _____Finger_____ _____Lakes_____ right now. I'm supposed to be in the _____Finger_____ _____Lakes_____ right now. I told them I was on a hike; snuck away to do this interview. I gotta get back pretty soon; they'll worry. People disappear in the _____Finger_____ _____Lakes._____

10. I just think it's insulting that Jan thinks we need this. And, apparently, judging from her _____outfit,_____ Jan aspires to be a _____whore._____

11. Bob Vance, _____Vance_____ _____Refrigeration._____

---

little kidney Jim lakes
death poop whore
urine garbage finger
beans small hair kid
Michael Vance Scott
outfit coke mung
refrigeration pulverize
expensive poop pretzel
paid lakes finger finger
lakes stones pretzel
lover

Fill in the Blank #2: Answers

__Blood__ alone moves the wheels of __history!__ Have you ever asked yourselves in an hour of __meditation,__ which everyone finds during the day. How long we have been striving for greatness? Not only the years we've been at war, the war of __work,__ but from the moment as a child when we realized that the world could be conquered. It has been a lifetime's struggle. A never-ending fight. I say to you and you'll understand that it is a __privilege__ to __fight!__ We are __warriors!__ Salesman of Northeastern Pennsylvania, I ask you once more rise and be worthy of this historical hour! No __revolution__ is worth anything unless it can defend itself. Some people will tell you __salesman__ is a bad word. They'll conjure up images of used car dealers and door to door __charlatans.__ This is our duty – to change their perception. I say salesmen... and __women__ of the world unite! We must never acquiesce for it is together, TOGETHER, THAT WE PREVAIL! We must never cede control the __motherland!__ For it is together that we prevail!

motherland   meditation
women   privilege   history
salesman   work
charlatans   fight   blood
revolution   Pennsylvania
warriors

Fill in the Blank #3: Answers

1. bye, bye, miss ___chair___
   ___model___ lady

2. you took my by the ___hand,___ made
   me a ___man,___ that one
   ___night!___

3. my horn can ___pierce___ the sky!

4. I dont wanna ___work,___ I just wanna
   bang on this ___mug___ all day

5. Hey Mr. Scott, whatcha gonna do,
   whatcha gonna do make our ___dreams___ ___come___ ___true___

6. Learn your rules, you better learn your rules, if you don't, you'll be
   ___eaten___ in your ___sleep___

7. You meet some ___friends,___ you tie some ___yarn___

8. Lazy ___Scranton,___ the Electric City they call it that 'cause of the
   ___electricity___

9. The city's laid out from east to ___west___ and our public
   ___parks___ and libraries are truly the ___best___

10. Call ___poison___ ___control___ if you're bit by a spider, but check th
    it's covered by your healthcare provider

11. Plenty of space in the parking lot, but the ___little___ ___cars___
    go in the ___compact___ spot!

best   night   poison
dreams   parks   cars
work   yarn   west   sleep
eaten   come   true   hand
electricity   man   compact
control   pierce   little
Scranton   mug   model
friends   chair

Fill in the Blank #4: Answers

<table>
<tr><td>Pam</td><td>Andy</td><td>Angela</td></tr>
<tr><td>Kevin</td><td>Jim</td><td>Gumby</td></tr>
<tr><td>Oscar</td><td>America</td><td>Creed</td></tr>
<tr><td>everybody</td><td colspan="2">Meredith</td></tr>
<tr><td>Stanley</td><td>Oscar</td><td>Dwight</td></tr>
</table>

1.   ___Jim,___ you're 6'11 and you weigh 90 pounds, ___Gumby___ has a better body than you.

2.   ___Dwight,___ you're a kiss ass. Boom. Roasted.

3.   ___Pam,___ you failed art school. Boom. Roasted.

4.   ___Meredith,___ you've slept with so many guys you're starting to look like one.

5.   ___Kevin,___ I can't decide between a fat joke and a dumb joke.

6.   ___Creed,___ you're teeth called, your breath stinks.

7.   Where's ___Angela?___ Whoa there you are, I didn't see you there behind that grain of rice.

8.   ___Stanley,___ you crush your wife during sex and your heart sucks.

9.   ___Oscar,___ you're gay.

10. ___Andy,___ Cornell called, they think you suck. And you're gayer than ___Oscar.___

.   Alright ___everybody,___ you know I kid, you know I kid. You guys are the reason I went into the paper business, so, uh, goodnight, God bless, God bless ___America,___ and get home safe.

Fill in the Blank #5: Answers

1. No Dwight, not the good ___peanut___
   ___butter.___ People are going to get
   mad.

2. ___Pizza.___ Great equalizer.

3. "Guys, ___beef!___ It's what's for
   dinner! Who wants some ___man___
   ___meat?"___ "I do! I want some
   ___man___ ___meat!"___

4. No ___mustard!___ Just... eat it. Eat it,
   Phyllis. Dip it in the water so it will
   slide down your gullet more easily.

5. Somebody making ___soup?___

6. And we are spoiled because we throw out perfectly good ___tiramisu___
   because it has a little tiny hair on it.

7. Last night I ordered a ___pizza___ by myself and I ate it over the
   sink like a rat.

8. I am on the third day of my cleanse diet. All I have to do is drink
   ___maple___ ___syrup,___ lemon juice, ___cayenne___ ___pepper___ and
   water for all three meals.

9. It's never too early for ice cream, Jim. But we didn't have any
   ___ice___ ___cream,___ so this is ___mayonnaise___ and black
   ___olives.___

10. Yes, I can do that. For, um, for two ___tacos,___ we'd probably need
    about what 20... $20? Or $25? $20?

11. I just want to lie on the beach and eat ___hot___ ___dogs.___
    That's all I've ever wanted.

12. I'll make a reservation. No, no. Let me cook for you. ___Cauliflower___ and
    noodles. Baked ___potato___ on the side.

13. Oh Angela, those ___brownies___ have ___walnuts___ in them and I think
    Kevin's allergic to ___walnuts.___ You're allergic to ___walnuts,___ right
    Kevin?

---

tiramisu pizza syrup
hot soup dogs peanut
potato walnuts pepper
beef pizza brownies
cayenne cauliflower
man walnuts cream
butter meat
mayonnaise mustard
walnuts ice man tacos
maple olives meat

Fill in the Blank #6: Answers

1. Nobody ever helped me. I had to do it myself. Even the ___doctor___ ___didn't___ ___know!___

2. I want my sugar free ___cookie,___ and then I want a ___sugar___ cookie.

3. It's um, it's really for anybody with a dream and a belief in ___magic___ and a little extra time after ___school.___

4. Please don't ___smell___ me Michael.

5. Nah, I wouldn't have done it if it wasn't for the discount ___paper.___ There's not a lot of ___fruit___ in those ___looms.___

6. She's been sick for some time. Thank you for asking, no one asks about ___Sprinkles.___

7. Eventually he'll figure it out, when their kids have giant heads and ___beet-stained___ teeth.

8. I want pie. I want ___peach___ pie.

9. I feel ___weak___ today. Felt much ___stronger___ yesterday. Like Benjamin Button in reverse.

10. Oh, hello Mater. Good news: I've married. ___Tell___ Fater.

smell know sugar
doctor Fater stronger
weak fruit sprinkles
paper peach tell
looms beet-stained
magic didn't school
cookie

Jumble Answers

1. Last Names

Original words: **palmer, martinez, schrute, martin, howard, kapoor, beesley, philbin, scott, vance, halpert, bernard, bratton, malone**

Final word or phrase: **levinson**

2. Michael Scott

Original words: **carol, best boss, gary, splenda, magic, sebring, holly, date mike, ping, beyonce, hockey, mykonos, condo, manager, fun jeans**

Final word or phrase: **You dont know me, you've just seen my penis.**

3. Robert California

Original words: **ceo, marmalade, divorce, susan, basil, bert, floria, squash, creep, gymnast, sabre, bob kazamakis**

Final word or phrase: **I'm the fucking lizard king!**

4. Oscar Martinez

Original words: **ice skate, yoga, lexus, yolo, warehouse guy, gil, mexican, kevin, finer things club, gay, democrat, calm, rational, accountant, senator**

Final word or phrase: **oscar mayer weiner lover**

5. The Dinner Party

Original words: **candles, wine, ossobuco, plasma, celebrity, dundie, babe, that one night, condo, flooded, polic**

Final word or phrase: **oaky after-birth**

6. Andy Bernard

Original words: **ace, buzz, nard dog, rich, cornell, boat, dork, bowtie, angry, a cappella**

Final word or phrase: **beer me that disc**

7. Gabe Lewis

Original words: **susan, japan, glee, sabre, tall, klutz, erin, horror, atheist**

Final word or phrase: **longest baby in the hospital**

8. Nellie Bertram

Original words: **sabre, crass, poland, adopt, drake, bold, toby, rude, english, red, magician, skirt, tacos**

Final word or phrase: **everybody told me if i moved to america, i'd be murdered**

Extracurriculars: Answers

1.	c	Michael	a.	yoga
2.	g	Phyllis	b.	community theatre
3.	d	Pam	c.	magic camp
4.	j	Dwight	d.	volleyball
5.	e	Jim	e.	bicycling
6.	b	Andy	f.	softball
7.	i	Toby	g.	bowling
8.	f	Darryl	h.	music
9.	h	Kevin	i.	writing
10.	a	Oscar	j.	karate

Match the Middle Name: Answers

1.	a	Kelly	a.	Rajani Ghana
2.	d	Andy	b.	Bailey
3.	i	Pam	c.	Susan
4.	g	Erin	d.	Baines
5.	b	Ryan	e.	Kurt
6.	c	Gabe	f.	Gary
7.	e	Dwight	g.	Erin
8.	f	Michael	h.	Noelle
9.	h	Angela	i.	Morgan

Brother From Another Mother: Answers

1.	j	Michael	a.	Rachel
2.	h	Dwight	b.	Walter
3.	g	Darryl	c.	Reed
4.	i	Toby	d.	Tom
5.	c	Erin	e.	Tiffany
6.	d	Jim	f.	Kenny
7.	b	Andy	g.	Gwenyth
8.	e	Kelly	h.	Fannie
9.	f	Roy	i.	Rory
10.	a	Angela	j.	a fake brother who steals your jeans

Their Other Jobs: Answers

1.	d	Ryan	a.	Osprey Paper
2.	a	Danny	b.	beauty pageant contestant
3.	f	Daryll	c.	Staples
4.	b	Angela	d.	bowling alley
5.	g	Josh	e.	drummer in a cover band
6.	j	Jan	f.	Athlead
7.	n	Kevin	g.	Staples
8.	m	Michael	h.	Taco Bell Express
9.	l	Dwight	i.	bar owner
10.	c	Dwight	j.	Scranton White Pages
11.	h	Erin	k.	fake ID business owner
12.	k	Creed	l.	bed and breakfast owner
13.	e	Kevin	m.	Men's Warehouse
14.	o	Roy	n.	bar owner
15.	i	Danny	o.	gravel company owner

Name that Dundie Winner: Answers

1.	l	Kevin	a.	Moving On Up Award
2.	g	Pam	b.	Worst Salesman of the Year
3.	f	Dwight	c.	Tight-Ass Award
4.	b	Oscar	d.	Hottest in the Office (Multiple Years)
5.	h	Stanley	e.	Bushiest Beaver Award
6.	d	Ryan	f.	Promising Assistant Manager Award
7.	a	Daryll	g.	Whitest Sneakers Award
8.	k	Kelly	h.	Diabetes Award
9.	e	Phyllis	i.	Doobie Doobie Pothead Stoner of the Year Award
10.	j	Toby	j.	Extreme Repulsiveness Award
11.	i	Andy	k.	Spicy Curry Award
12.	c	Angela	l.	Don't Go in There After Me Award
13.	m	Jim	m.	Best Dad Award

Match the Ex: Answers

1.	m	Pam	a.	Jessica
2.	h	Jim	b.	Kathy
3.	j	Kelly	c.	Kelly
4.	e	Darryl	d.	Robert Lipton
5.	a	Andy	e.	Val
6.	k	Oscar	f.	Gabe
7.	i	Michael	g.	Stacy
8.	n	Holly	h.	Katie
9.	g	Kevin	i.	Donna
10.	b	Toby	j.	Darryl
11.	l	Stanley	k.	Gil
12.	c	Ryan	l.	Cynthia
13.	d	Angela	m.	Roy
14.	f	Erin	n.	AJ

Match
the Ailment: Answers

1.	k	Meredith	a. Used to be in an iron lung
2.	f	Andy	b. Cooked Foot
3.	j	Darryl	c. Scoliosis
4.	l	DeAngelo	d. Kidney stones
5.	e	Meredith	e. Rabies
6.	c	Phylis	f. Irritable Bowel Syndrome
7.	a	Creed	g. Anal Fissures
8.	b	Michael	h. High blood pressure
9.	i	Angela	i. Dermatitis
10.	g	Kevin	j. Soy Allergy
11.	h	Jim	k. Dairy Allergy
12.	d	Dwight	l. Peanut Allergy

Answer: Name The Nickname

1.	h	Gabe	a. C-Span
2.	d	Stanley	b. Nard Dog
3.	m	Phyllis	c. Big Pregs
4.	i	Michael	d. Stankley
5.	c	Pam	e. Mr. Rogers
6.	g	Ryan	f. Little Kevin
7.	e	Daryll	g. Rye-Bread
8.	a	Oscar	h. Birdman
9.	b	Andy	i. Caleb Crawdad
10.	l	Dwight	j. Monkey
11.	n	Jim	k. Hillary Rodham Clinton
12.	f	Philip	l. Possum
13.	k	Jan	m. Mother Goose
14.	j	Angela	n. Tuna

Halloween Costumes: Answers

1.	f	Pam	a. Just Dracula (not Blackula)
2.	l	Erin	b. Nancy Reagan
3.	j	Toby	c. Uncle Sam
4.	k	Dwight	d. Jesse Pinkman
5.	c	Oscar	e. Lady Gaga
6.	d	Ryan	f. Dr. Cinderella
7.	i	Creed	g. OJ Simpson
8.	a	Darryl	h. Snookie
9.	h	Kelly	i. Osama Bin Laden
10.	e	Gabe	j. Hugh Hefner
11.	g	Michael	k. Sith Lord (not a monk)
12.	b	Angela	l. Wendy from Wendy's

Whose Kid?: Answers

1.	d	Cece	a. David Wallace
2.	a	Teddy	b. Robert California
3.	e	Sasha	c. Meredith
4.	i	Drake	d. Jim and Pam
5.	c	Jake	e. Toby
6.	f	Philip L.	f. Dwight
7.	b	Bert	g. Jan
8.	h	Jada	h. Daryll
9.	j	Melissa	i. Ryan
10.	g	Astrid	j. Stanley

Answers: Creed's Crossword

Across

2. _____ Charles Schneider
6. You have more fun as a follower, but you make more _____ as a leader.
8. I've been involved in a number of _____, both as a leader and a follower.
9. quabity assuance, but to a normal person
10. name of Creed's blog
12. smells like death

Down

1. pattern of thievery
3. band name
4. soup kitchen's featured item on Thursdays that Cree donates his Casino money to
5. Creed claims to have been treated with one of these a child
7. what Creed sells out of the trunk of his car to young people
11. Hey, did one of you tell Stanley I have asthma? Because I don't, and if it gets out, they won't let me ___

Answers: Clark and Pete's Crossword

ross

2. Clark brings back an espresso maker from this Campania Region holiday destination from his travels with Jan.

4. Jan ensures Clark has one of this before taking him abroad.

5. Pete's in-office love interest

8. they both grow a mustache with Toby for this

10. Andy hires this ex-girlfriend, to get back at Pete

12. Clark's nickname, not 'Fart'

13. Clark act like a creep and convinces Erin to audition or this role

Down

1. Clark's large inner ears make him particularly adept at this activity

3. Both are hired as _____ _____ representatives when Kelly and Ryan move to Ohio.

6. Pete's nickname

7. When Dwight and Clark pretend to be father and son, Dwight accuses Clark of being this type of collector.

9. movie that Pete knows, line for line

11. Pete is a native of this maple place

Answers: Darryl's Crossword

Across

4. he breaks this container after this interview with Athlead, resulting in the death of the contents

6. 'Look, just be straight with me, man. You can be _____ with Matt, just be straight with me.'

9. Darryl sells this doll to Toby for $400

11. He works as the _____ of the warehouse.

12. Michael's practical joke ends with him falling and busting this body part

Down

1. shared religion with Pam

2. Michael whips out his negotiation techniques when Darryl asks for a modest raise of _____ _____.

3. ex-girlfriend, 'access your uncrazy side'

5. Darryl develops an allergy to this, which he says is everything

7. material of the gloves that Darryl intends for Val, b_ diverts to Nate

8. 'What'd I tell you about building forts in my _____

10. Daughter's name

Answers: One Liners Crossword

Across

4. Well, happy birthday, _____. Sorry your party's so lame.

6. If you pray enough, you can change yourself into a _____ _____.

8. Steer clear Big Tuna. Head for _____ _____.

11. I'm forced to go to the American Girl store and order clothes for large _____ _____.

13. You can't fire me, I don't work in this ___!

14. 'Hi, I'm date Mike. Nice to _____ _____'

Down

1. I am one of the few people who looks hot eating a _____.

2. Sorry I annoyed you with my _____.

3. The trick is to _____ the onions.

5. I'm not superstitious, but I am a little _____.

7. Crazy world, lotta _____.

9. Monkey see, monkey do. Monkey ____ ____ _____ you.

10. I want to be wined, dined, and _____-_____.

12. Gum's gotten _____ lately. Have you noticed?

Answers: Stanley Hudson's Crossword

1 bio-feedback machine
2 toaster toaster
3 stanley the manly
4 crossword puzzles
5 diabetes
6 pretzel day
7 teri
8 the black panthers
9 lighthouse
10 florida stanley

Across

3. Michael's nickname for Stanley
4. What he would rather be doing than working
6. A day Stanley likes
8. A movement Stanley was involved in when he was 'eating whatever he wanted'
9. Stanley would like a decommissioned one to live in
10. Who do you want on your Florida team?

Down

1. Alerts Stanley when his stress goes up
2. A doubled up kitchen appliance
5. Stanley once got a Dundie award for being the face this debilitating disease
7. That person? That woman is not my mother. She is step mother.'

Answer: The Injury Crossword

cross

1. celestial body, body part
2. breakfast meat of the buttled
7. superior quality of the Prism Duro-Sport
8. elbow plus wall bump equals a
10. actor with the rare disability of growing into a man overnight
11. country of origin of the website that sells cheap songs
13. town where the gas station was yamless

Down

1. other superior quality of the Prism Duro-Sport
3. sweet medium in which to hide crushed aspirin
4. Michael's margarine of preference
5. more serious than a foot injury
6. breakroom snack, just go for it
9. word Dwight is seen typing over and over
12. I wanna clamp Michael's _____ in a George Foreman grill.

Answers: General Knowledge Crossword

4. Kevin's magic number

Across

4. Kevin's magic number
5. Kevin and Creed's Halloween costume
6. the worst thing about prison
8. Oscar's dogs name
9. Who Michael thinks he sees in NYC
10. This person let Dwight steer the boar
11. Bob Vance, Vance _____.
12. What Michael wants in his scotch

Down

1. has been paid $150,000 over 20 years by Dwight for
hobby
2. Andy's alma mater
3. social group where no paper, plastic, or work talk is
allowed
7. owns a dog named Ruby, who may be dead

Answers: Schrute Farms

cross

2. co-owner of the farm
6. This website is the lifeblood of the agritourism industry
8. themed room, water
10. themed room, country
12. the most attractive beets
13. the farmhouse has nine of these
14. themed room, dark

Down

1. rich in folate, this crop is grown on Dwight's Farm
3. original acreage
4. who Angela actually marries here
5. where Dwight's farmhouse bathroom is located
7. era in which the Battle of Schrute Farms was fought
9. 'So what kind of farming you into, huh? You more of a fruit man or a _____ _____?'
11. who Angela plans to marry here

The Party Planning Committee

Across

4. Baby Shower M&Ms-girl name
5. Historic person who attend's Phyllis' Bridal Shower
6. This person blackmailed her way to become head of the committee
7. Themes of the rival Christmas party thrown by Karen and Pam
8. To celebrate Dunder Mifflin Infinity, not a midday meal
11. bad dessert choice for Meredith's surprise party, given her dairy allergy

Down

1. Happens only once every billion years
2. Theme of the party that featured hummus plates, pita triangles
3. Baby Shower M&Ms-boy name
9. Welcome party for this person was bad on purpose, carrot cake, magician
10. Eventually shut down by this character

Answers: Jim and Pam Crossword

cross

Across

4. honeymoon inside joke, other couple
6. state of marriage
7. what cartoon jim becomes, post radioactive bear bite
8. Jim purchased these at Toby's party before Andy swooped in
9. type of flooring in Jim's parent's house
10. vessel of inside jokes, love
11. favorite yogurt of half the couple
13. location of proposal
14. honeymoon location

Down

1. Angela's game, played between Jim and Pam's desk
2. once a spiritual experience, now kitschy; place.
3. vessel of love, boat
5. little ladybug Halpert
12. Named after grandfather (or favorite cat)

Answer Key:
Help Find Michael's Moppy Place

Answer Key: Help Erin Find Her Birth Parents

Answer Key: Help Kevin Find His Toupee

Answer Key: Help Phyllis Finish Her Mittens

Help Andy Become the A Capela Star of his Dreams

Answer: Help Meredith Find her PhD

Help Roy Find His True, Non-Pam Love

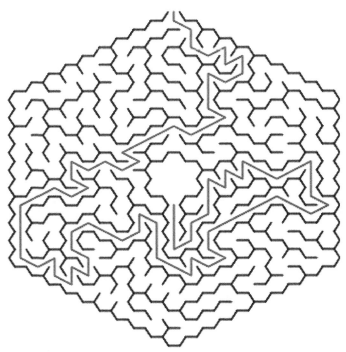

Jan Levinson, I presume?

(word search grid)

SERENITY BY JAN · HUNTER · GOULD
FOLIAGE · ANNE TAYLOR · CHILI'S
JAMAICA · CHINESE FOOD · ASTRID
HOSPITAL SUPPLIES · OSSO BUCO · BOOB ENHANCEMENT
GODZILLARY · ICE QUEEN

Toby

(word search grid)

PRINCESS UNICORN · COSTA RICA · EVIL SNAIL
ZIPLINE · STRANGLER · MOVEMBER
HR · JURY DUTY · CHAD FLENDERMAN
DUNDERBALL · SASHA · SEMINARY
DIVORCED · CAPRESE · SEXY TOBY

The Cats of Angela Martin

(word search grid)

SPRINKLES · GARBAGE · BANDIT
PRINCESS LADY · MR. ASH · PETALS
COMSTOCK · EMBER · MILKYWAY
DIANE · LUMPY · PHILIP
TINKIE · CRINKLEPUSS · BANDIT TWO
PAWLICK BAGGINS · LADY ARAGORN

The Warehouse

(word search grid)

ROY · HIDE · LONNY
DARRYL · FRANK · GLENN
MICHAEL · MADGE · NATE
PHILIP · VAL · JERRY
MATT

The Works

SWEET GLAZE
WHITE CHOCOLATE
CARAMEL DIP
MARSHMALLOW
COCONUTS
SPRINKLES

CINNAMON SUGAR
FUDGE
MINT CHIP
NUTS
PEANUT BUTTER
DRIZZLE
COTTON CANDY BITS

CHOCOLATE
M&MS
CHOCOLATE CHIP
TOFFEE NUTS
OREOS
POWDERED SUGAR

Meredith

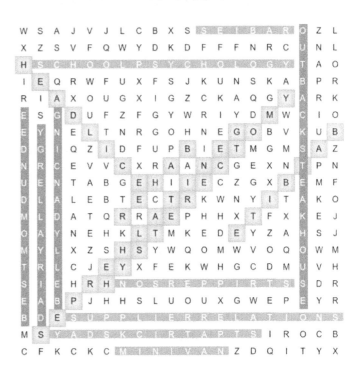

SUPPLIER RELATIONS
RABIES
MINIVAN
REHAB
GENITAL HERPES

DAIRY ALLERGY
STRIPPER SON
HYSTERECTOMY
OUTBACK STEAKHOUSE
SCHOOL PSYCHOLOGY

BELLYDANCING
BAT BITE
ST. PATRICK'S DAY
BEST MOM DUNDEE
HEAD LICE

Threat Level Midnight

GOLDENFACE
DWIGT
SCREENPLAY
THE SCARN

MICHAEL SCARN
ROBOT BUTLER
ALL STAR GAME
FUNKY CAT

HOCKEY
CHEROKEE JACK
FBI
MOP THE ICE

Cameos

IDRIS ELBA
WARREN BUFFET
JIM CARREY
JACK BLACK
WILL ARNETT

STEPHEN COLBERT
RAY ROMANO
AMY ADAMS
JESSICA ALBA
CHRISTIAN SLATER

JOAN CUSACK
WILL FERRELL
JOSH GROBAN
RICKY GERVAIS
KATHY BATES

The Scranton Strangler

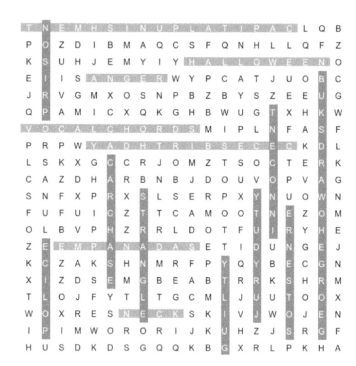

GEORGE HOWARD SKUB
HALLOWEEN
PRISON
GUILTY
CAR CHASE
VOCAL CHORDS

JURY DUTY
EMPANADAS
NECK
INNOCENT
POLICE

CECE'S BIRTHDAY
ERNESTO'S
ANGER
STRANGLE
CAPITAL PUNISHMENT

Break Me Off A Piece of That...

CHRYSLER CAR
SNICKERS BAR
HAIR FOR MEN
FANCY FEAST

FOOTBALL CREAM
GREY POUPON
POISON GAS

LUMBER TAR
CLAUDE VAN DAMME
NUTRASWEET

Minor Characters

BRIAN
HANK TATE
BRANDON
ASTRID
BRENDA
LEO AND GINO

JUSTINE
MR. BROWN
ELIZABETH THE STRIPPER
JAKE PALMER
BILLY MERCHANT
IRENE

THE SCRANTON STRANGLER
THE PRINCE FAMILY
VIKRAM
NURSE CYNTHIA
RAVI
CATHY

The Regulars

STANLEY
PAM
ANDY
ANGELA
ROY
TOBY
ERIN

DWIGHT
JIM
KEVIN
OSCAR
JAN
CREED

MICHAEL
RYAN
MEREDITH
PHYLLIS
KELLY
DARRYL

GREAT SCOTT!

PRODUCTIONS

Made in the USA
Monee, IL
12 December 2020